EPIGRAMS AND THE FOREST

BEN JONSON was born in 1572, probably in London. His father died shortly after he was born and his mother married a bricklayer. Jonson himself was briefly apprenticed to a brick-layer. He attended Westminster School, served with the army in the Netherlands and married. By 1597 he was employed as an actor-writer. In 1598 he was imprisoned for killing a fellow-actor, and narrowly escaped hanging. From 1599 Jonson began to write satirical comedies, some of which brought him into conflict with the authorities. He was imprisoned on a number of occasions, although he also benefited from royal patronage and wrote masques for court performance. In 1603 his first son died of the plague. Some of Jonson's greatest works were written from this period: *Volpone* (1606), *The Alchemist* (1610) and *Bartholomew Fair* (1614). In 1616 Jonson published the First Folio of his *Works*, including *Epigrams* and *The Forest*, and he was granted a royal pension. Jonson did not experience such successes again, though he continued to write. In 1623 a fire destroyed his library, and in 1628 he suffered a stroke, but he remained an important influence on younger poets. Jonson died in 1637 and was buried in Westminster Abbey.

RICHARD DUTTON has been Professor of English at Lancaster University (UK) and is currently Professor of English at Ohio State University. He has published widely on Renaissance literature and edited a number of texts from the period, including *Jacobean Civic Pageants* (1995), *'Women Beware Women' and Other Plays* by Thomas Middleton (1999) and Jonson's *Epicene* and *Volpone*. He is the editor (with Jean Howard) of four volumes of *Companions to Shakespeare's Works* (2002). Richard Dutton's anthology of the *Selected Writings* of Philip Sidney is published in the Fyfield series.

FyfieldBooks aim to make available some of the great classics of British and European literature in clear, affordable formats, and to restore often neglected writers to their place in literary tradition.

FyfieldBooks take their name from the Fyfield elm in Matthew Arnold's 'Scholar Gypsy' and 'Thyrsis'. The tree stood not far from the village where the series was originally devised in 1971.

> *Roam on! The light we sought is shining still.*
> *Dost thou ask proof? Our tree yet crowns the hill,*
> *Our Scholar travels yet the loved hill-side*

from 'Thyrsis'

BEN JONSON

Epigrams and The Forest

Edited with an introduction by
RICHARD DUTTON

Fyfield*Books*

CARCANET

First published in Great Britain in 1984 by
Carcanet Press Limited
Alliance House
Cross Street
Manchester M2 7AQ

This impression 2003

A CIP catalogue record for this book is available from the British Library
ISBN 1 85754 705 5

The publisher acknowledges financial assistance from
the Arts Council of England

Printed and bound in England by SRP Ltd, Exeter

Contents

THE FOREST

For Tom

Introduction

Ben Jonson is a familiar figure, and rather larger than life. The strikingly convincing portrait stares at us from the wall of the National Portrait Gallery, while his own writings help to flesh out the picture; 'On My Picture Left in Scotland' comments ruefully on 'my mountain belly and rocky face', while the Induction to the play, *The Staple of News*, describes him among the actors, 'rolling himself up and down like a tun'. Fortuitously too, when Jonson undertook an epic walk from London to Edinburgh and back in 1618-19, he stayed with the Scots poet, William Drummond, whose account of their *Conversations* survives, offering a wealth of insight into Jonson's life, character and opinions. It is perhaps not the fairest record of Jonson we might have, since Jonson appears not to have known that his words were being taken down and was all too often in his cups ('drink...is one of the elements in which he liveth', his host noted sourly); and the prim Scot was not the man best suited to appreciate his overpowering English guest. His cool final assessment of Jonson, for example — 'a great lover and praiser of himself, a contemner and scorner of others, given rather to lose a friend than a jest...' — perhaps tells us as much about the differences in their temperaments as it does about the real Jonson. Nevertheless, it is difficult to believe that the authentic Jonson does not sometimes speak to us, directly and memorably, through Drummond's words: 'That Donne, for not keeping of accent, deserved hanging'; 'He esteemeth Donne the first poet in the world, in some things'; 'That Shakespeare wanted art'; 'He beat Marston, and took his pistol from him'; 'He married a wife, who was a shrew yet honest'; 'He hath consumed a whole night in lying looking to his great toe, about which he hath seen Tartars and Turks, Romans and Carthaginians, fight in his imagination'; 'Of all styles he loved most to be named honest, and hath of that an hundred letters so naming him'; and so forth.

11

All this helps us to feel that we know the personality behind the writings and the career. The career, too, is well enough known, at least in outline. Jonson was born, probably in 1572, probably in London. His father died about a month before he was born and his mother was shortly remarried, to a bricklayer. Jonson himself was briefly apprenticed as a bricklayer, which he considered a demeaning trade; it was something enemies later would never let him forget. He was also, however, apparently able to study at Westminster School for a time, under the great scholar William Camden (see *Epigrams*, XIV) and this laid the basis for his considerable learning. After brief service with the army in the Netherlands, and marriage (1594) to the 'shrew' Anne Lewis, Jonson became involved in the theatrical world; by 1597 he was employed as an actor-writer by the entrepreneur Philip Henslowe, and that year (his first recorded brush with authority) he was imprisoned for part-writing of a lost satirical play, *The Isle of Dogs*. The following year his play *Every Man in his Humour* was performed by the Lord Chamberlain's Men; according to popular tradition, Shakespeare was instrumental in getting it staged. But also in 1598 Jonson killed his fellow-actor Gabriel Spencer in a duel, and only escaped hanging by pleading benefit of clergy; while in prison he was converted to Roman Catholicism and was thereafter 'twelve years a papist' (Drummond). Between 1599 and 1601 he helped create a new style of dramatic 'comicall satyre', with plays like *Every Man out of his Humour* and *The Poetaster*, some of which were involved in the so-called War of the Theatres. In 1603 his first extant tragedy was a failure on the stage, and also got him into trouble with the authorities: 'he was called before the (Privy) Council for his *Sejanus*, and accused both of popery and treason by (the Earl of Northampton)' (Drummond). In this year too, Jonson's first son, Benjamin died of the plague (see *Epigrams*, XLV); Jonson was away from home when it happened but, before hearing the news 'he saw in a vision his eldest son…appear unto him with the mark of a bloody cross on his forehead, as if he had been cutted with a sword' (Drummond).

In 1605 Jonson wrote his first royal masque, *The Masque of Blackness*, which was staged by the great architect and theatrical designer, Inigo Jones. They collaborated frequently thereafter in the reign of James I, and between them developed the masque to a high art; but their partnership, although fruitful, was always fraught with artistic and professional jealousy, which eventually erupted in public; and while Jones retained favour under Charles I, Jonson on the whole did not. For much of his career, however, these royal commissions gave Jonson reasonable financial security, which enabled him largely to escape the treadmill of hack-writing and obsequious appeals for patronage which was the lot of so many of his contemporaries. 1605 was also a year in which he was again imprisoned, this time for his part with Marston and Chapman in the play *Eastward Ho*, which contained some pointedly anti-Scottish satire. (The King, of course, was a Scot.) 'The report was, that they should then have their ears cut, and noses' (Drummond); fortunately, it did not come to that. This was also the year of the Gunpowder Plot, with which Jonson was directly connected (see below).

1606 marked the beginning of the most fruitful period of Jonson's career, signalled by his first dramatic masterpiece, *Volpone*. *Epicoene* followed in 1609, *The Alchemist* in 1610, *Bartholomew Fair* in 1614, *The Devil is an Ass* in 1616. There was one notable failure — *Catiline*, his other extant tragedy, was hissed off the stage in 1611 — but on the whole it was a period of conspicuous success. Jonson marked this for himself in 1616 by publishing the First Folio of his *Works*; this was not simply a compilation of everything he had written but an opulent and carefully edited collection only of those plays by which he wanted to be remembered (up to, and defiantly including, *Catiline* but omitting collaborations and early hack work), all his masques to date and a few other significant commissions, and two extremely selective poem-sequences, *Epigrams* (which there had been plans to publish separately in

13

1612, but it is not clear if they came to fruition) and *The Forest*. Jonson was initially mocked for including plays, until then regarded only as popular entertainment, and not as art, in such a prestigious volume; but his own growing eminence helped change opinion and paved the way for the Shakespeare First Folio (with Jonson's own magnificent introductory poem) in 1623. The King also gave recognition in 1616 to Jonson's standing as a man of letters, in the form of a royal pension — making him in effect, if not in name, the first Poet Laureate. In 1619, after the trip to Scotland, he had the rare distinction of being given an Honorary MA from the University of Oxford. This period of success was also marked by two other significant events. Around 1610 Jonson returned to the Church of England; at his first reconciled communion 'he drank out all the full cup of wine'. The other matter also involved drink; in 1612-13 he went to France as tutor to the son of Sir Walter Raleigh. 'This youth, being knavishly inclined...caused him to be drunken, and dead drunk, so that he knew not where he was, thereafter laid him on a car, which he made to be drawn by pioneers through the streets, at every corner showing his governor stretched out, and telling them, that was a more lively image of the crucefix than any they had' (Drummond).

It is difficult not to read the rest of Jonson's career as a slow falling off from the heights of this period. He retired from the stage, in effect in 1616, and only returned in 1626 (with *The Staple of News*) when the death of James I lost him his regular masque-commission. It has been commonplace to dismiss the plays after 1625, in Dryden's term, as 'dotages'. This is not really fair, since they contain some new and interesting developments, but they were not generally received well at the time (*The New Inn*, 1629, was hissed off the stage, occasioning Jonson's bitter 'Ode to Himself' which begins, 'Come leave the loathed stage') and it would be difficult even now to argue that they are on a par with his best work. Circumstances also conspired against him. A fire in 1623 destroyed his library and, apparently, a number of works in progress. In 1628 he suffered a stroke which confined him to his bed for a time; that same year he was appointed City Chronologer to the City of London, but the appointment was revoked when he was unable or unwilling to produce what they wanted of him. In 1631 the old antagonism with Inigo Jones flared openly, and he received no royal commissions after that date. But the impression of unremitting decline is to some extent misleading, and is exacerbated by the fact that he did not live to see his later work carefully edited and selected in a Second Folio. In fact the masques continued to improve, at least up to the death of King James, and the non-dramatic verse shows no real falling-off, though it lacks the advantages of the careful focus which he had given to the *Epigrams* and *The Forest*. And for much of the time Jonson enjoyed an eminence in literary circles which rivals that of his better-chronicled namesake, Dr Johnson; at various taverns — most notably in the Apollo Room at the Devil Tavern — Jonson presided over the self-styled 'Tribe of Ben', a younger generation of poets who acknowledged him as their leader and who must increasingly have seen him as the last survivor of the great Elizabethan generation that flourished at the turn of the century — Shakespeare, Bacon, Donne, Raleigh — all of whom he had known. He died on 6 August 1637, and was duly buried in Westminster Abbey; plans for a splendid memorial fell through as the country slipped towards civil war. Instead there is a simple inscription, carved in stone: 'O rare Ben Jonson'.

The career and the personality, then, are familiar enough. Sadly, it is a familiarity which has bred, not so much contempt, as a kind of complacency about Jonson's writing, and particularly his non-dramatic verse. His poetry is, so the assumption goes, known, understood, weighed up: it has none of the compulsive panache or dramatic personality of Donne, or the intriguing enigma of Marvell. On the other hand, Jonson left nothing of the scale and obvious impressiveness of *The Faerie Queene* or *Paradise Lost*. The result is that he has come to be known as a poet of limitations, labelled as a moralist, a classicist, a satirist and an occasional poet — all terms with pejorative overtones. One ambition of this volume is to break through that complacency and to offer something of Jonson as he was to his contemporaries: an urgent and challenging figure. It is easy enough, of course, to point to individual poems that readers will find impressive: the moving restraint of 'On My First Daughter' and 'On My First Son' (*Epigrams*, XXII and XLV), the eloquence of 'To Penshurst' (*The Forest*, II); the grace and charm of the songs 'To Celia' (*The Forest*, V, VI, IX). But there is more to Jonson than the occasional impressive poem. The simple, often-ignored fact which this volume is designed to emphasize is that the best of Jonson's early verse was presented not as a random collection but as two deliberate and careful selections. They are meant to be read as poem-sequences, whether or not individual pieces were originally written with this in mind; these sequences are more structured, say, than Donne's *Songs and Sonnets* or even Shakespeare's *Sonnets*, analogous perhaps to George Herbert's *The Temple*. Within them, each individual piece takes on greater significance as it is appreciated in its assigned context.

'Rare poems', said Jonson, 'ask rare friends' (*Epigrams*, XCIV). The organization of the *Epigrams* is certainly such that it is not appreciated immediately; we find poems written perhaps as early as 1595 (putative date of the death of his first daughter) and perhaps as late as 1610, in an apparently arbitrary mixture of praise and censure, elegy and commentary. We may find a clue as to what Jonson expects of us in words he prefaced to *Catiline* which, like these 'ripest of my studies', was dedicated to the great literary patron, Philip, Earl of Pembroke: 'The commendation of good things may fall within a many, their approbation but in a few; for the most commend out of affection, self-tickling, an easiness or imitation: but men judge only out of knowledge. That is the trying faculty.' Knowledge here is not a simple accumulation of facts: it is an active and prescriptive virtue, incorporating discrimination and judgment. This is what gives the real edge, for example, to the closing line of 'To Mere English Censurer' (*Epigrams*, XVIII): 'Thy faith is all the knowledge that thou hast', just as it clinches the compliment to Sir Henry Goodyere (*Epigrams*, LXXXVI): 'It was a knowledge, that begat that love.' Knowledge, the 'trying faculty' is what these poems ask of their 'friends', for without it they will never really come to life.

To examine what this means in practice, let us examine a sequence of epigrams: LII to LVI, 'To Censorious Courtling', 'To Old-End Gatherer', 'On Chev'ril', 'To Francis Beaumont' and 'On Poet-Ape'. It is immediately apparent that the poem to Beaumont, the famous author, is in a different category from the others, which are addressed to anonymous or fictitious people; on the other hand, all the poems are linked in being about writing and the appreciation of writing. Courtling tries to hide his lack of judgment by only praising Jonson 'frostily'; Old-End Gatherer is a pathetic plagiarist; Cheveril (whose name means pliable leather) is a lawyer who accuses Jonson's verses of being libellous; Poet-Ape is a preposterous poetaster trying to forge a reputation from reworking other people's plays. Clearly Beaumont, whom Jonson praises, is located here as a riposte to the spurious writing, bad judgment and false esteem all around. The fact that the poem takes the form of a reply to a flattering verse-letter from Beaumont to Jonson lends this a personal edge, since Beaumont's eminence adds weight to Jonson's scorn of such characters who do not really understand him, or who perversely misinterpret him, or who plagiarize him. This small sequence is thus more than the sum of its parts: it is a continuing debate, and if we examine the poem to Beaumont in detail we may begin to doubt if it does not go further yet. How are we to take the 'religion' that Beaumont uses to Jonson, which makes him 'fear myself', or the 'indulgent thought thy pen drops forth'? Is Jonson, the master of verbal nuance, accusing Beaumont of being uncritically fulsome, even possibly a little condescending? When he asks 'What art is thine that so thy friend deceives?' are we still within the bounds of witty, paradoxical compliment, or have

17

things taken on a more critical edge? The key to the poem, as so often, is the closing couplet, where the crucial phrase 'For writing better' is placed with masterly ambiguity, in such a way that it refers both to Beaumont and to Jonson himself. One might interpret this as sly satire, Jonson coolly putting Beaumont in his place while seeming to compliment him; but I suggest that it is less devious than that. The mutual compliments of the two writers do beg the question of which of them is, in reality, the better poet; Jonson remains within the bounds of friendship, but it is an adult friendship which does not scruple to hint at reservations, with the kinds of doubts about styles and standards which equals, perhaps, ought to share. Even the great Beaumont must suffer the same critical scrutiny as 'Poet-Ape'; compliments must not be lightly given for friendship or for reputation. The net effect of this must surely be to broaden and intensify the whole sequence of poems which focus on the nature of writing and judgment. It is not simply a matter of the good dispelling the bad, but of a need for constant standards, for what Jonson calls knowledge.

The need for knowledge is not confined to the appreciation of poetry (which Jonson often uses as a metaphor for understanding generally) but applies to the whole range of human activity, as we can see in the poems that follow immediately (LVIII to LXV): 'To Groom Idiot', 'On Spies', 'To William, Lord Mounteagle', 'To Fool, or Knave', 'To Fine Lady Would-Be', 'To Robert, Earl of Salisbury', 'To the Same', 'To My Muse'. Jonson continues the debate on literary judgment in LVIII, LXI and LXV, but also introduces disparate material which focuses on the figures of Lord Mounteagle and the Earl of Salisbury. The former was the Catholic peer who was supposedly forewarned of the Gunpowder Plot and whose revelation of this to the authorities (i.e. Salisbury) led to the eleventh-hour discovery of the plotters. History has long been divided on the Gunpowder Plot: was there a real secret conspiracy only discovered at the last minute, or was it a put-up job, devised by Salisbury to discredit the Catholics and cement his own power under James I? Jonson's praise of Mounteagle and the modest Salisbury seems to imply that he held the former view; but again, closer inspection raises doubts. There is some evidence to suggest that Jonson was employed by Salisbury *before* the discovery of the Plot (he certainly was immediately afterwards) and that he was in the company of the plotters: a double agent? Whatever the case, the little squib 'On Spies' adjacent to the eulogy of Mounteagle raises uncomfortable speculations. Is Jonson hinting that in reality the national hero too was a spy, another double agent? And why should Jonson follow his two poems to Salisbury with 'To My Muse' which begins 'Away, and leave me, thou thing most abhorr'd / That hast betray'd me to a worthless lord'? It is difficult to resist the implication that the 'worthless lord' is in fact Salisbury. The scenario now looks very different, with Jonson raising critical doubts about those he seems to praise. We must remember that it would have been impossible for Jonson, in the political conditions of the day, to state such doubts openly, and even this cryptic prompting to the alert reader would be dangerous enough. As it is, Jonson blends necessary caution with his chosen poetic strategy, to involve his readers in a process of critical enquiry.

This perhaps leaves two questions for a modern reader: first, is it not hypocritical of Jonson to write poems in praise of men he does not respect, however much he may hedge them with qualifications; and secondly, what is 'To Fine Lady Would-Be' doing in this sequence? Jonson has his own answer to the first question; 'To My Muse' ends: 'Whoe'er is rais'd, / For worth he has not, he is tax'd, not prais'd.' Jonson depicts the ideal, the man as he should be; it is for the individual to live up to that. He is concerned, in effect, to teach by praising — the literal obverse of his role as a satirist. And we as readers need to bear in mind the possible discrepancy between the public appearance that Jonson celebrates and the human reality that lies beneath. Fine Lady Would-Be may be here to remind us of that possible discrepancy; on the other hand, the organization of the *Epigrams* is cryptic, suggestive, allusive, and there is not always a straightforward explanation for specific details. She may be here as a feint, a distraction from over-easy connections and conclusions which might prove politically sensitive. And one other possibility cannot be ignored: that she is an allusion to her namesake in *Volpone*, a play written within three months of the Gunpowder Plot, and itself full of plots and discoveries. So Jonson's method opens up new questions and possibilities, in intriguing and engrossing ways: as much as Donne's conceits or Marvell's paradoxes, Jonson's poetry offers us an emotional and intellectual challenge.

This remains true of *The Forest* but, inventive strategist that he is, Jonson has changed the tactics and the terms of the challenge. This collection is essentially concerned with a single issue, 'the virtuous life'; its organization is less cryptic than that of the *Epigrams* but, given its size, no less varied. The majority of the poems, and the weightiest, are exemplary, offering images of virtue, or exhortations to it, in the examples of a select band of named individuals: between them they confront a number of overlapping major issues: virtue and vice, love and life, court and country, marriage and manhood, poetry and death. Significantly, behind almost all of them stands the figure of 'godlike Sidney', Sir Philip Sidney, the Elizabethan paragon — brother of the present lord of Penshurst, uncle of the wife of Sir Herbert Wroth, father of the Countess of Rutland, uncle of Sir William Sidney. In Jonson's verse, their lives are (or are encouraged to be) tributes to the great example he gave; they in turn become secondary examples to us, the readers — and Jonson's verse takes on the daunting task of supplying for us what personal knowledge and family association have supplied for them.

But these poems in themselves only offer the reader one kind of approach or perspective; to offset this Jonson has interwoven poems with radically different forms and apparent themes, though ultimately they all refer to the same central

20

question of the virtuous life. For example, he opens the collection not, as might be expected, with the self-evident substance of 'To Penshurst', but with a wry reflection on being too old for love poetry (and an implicit 'apology' for his 'cold' moralizing). Yet four poems later he offers us one of the most seductive lyrics in the language ('Come my Celia, let us prove') and later still one of the most exquisite ('Drink to me only with thine eyes'). The turn-about is a wry admission that human passions and susceptibilities are less predictable than we may think, and less tractable than moralists may believe; even Jonson himself is not immune. These love lyrics, with their direct, sensuous apprehension of the world's delights and illusions, offer a very different perspective from the virtuous *exempla* around them. 'Come my Celia', like all true seduction poems, places the reader in the position of the besieged lady and confronts him/her with a hymn to sensuality; in *Volpone*, where the song first appeared, the force of the passionate logic is undercut by our knowledge that Bonario lurks in the wings, waiting to save Celia if her own virtue cannot. But we have no such assurance; we need all our wits to counter the plausible arguments. Do we notice the ambiguous use of 'may' ('while we *may*, the sports of love'), or an implicit Christian pun (sun/son in 'Suns that set may rise again'), or the echo of *Genesis* ('love's fruit to steal'), or indeed that Celia's name pointedly means 'heavenly one'? As so often, Jonson rounds on us in the closing couplet: 'To be taken, to be seen / These have crimes accounted been.' The barest statement of the amoral creed is also a reminder of our responsibilities as 'knowledgeable' readers; the more *we* 'take' and 'see' ('may', 'sun', 'fruit') the more a whole dimension of moral accountability opens up, and the more we may distinguish 'crimes' from innocent pleasures.

The need to 'take' and 'see' is not confined to the nuances within each poem, but also to the arrangement of the sequence as a whole. 'Come my Celia' follows an intriguing antithesis, 'To the World', an unusual monologue subtitled 'A Farewell

21

for a Gentlewoman, Virtuous and Noble'. Similarly 'Drink to me only', that charming celebration of love's intoxicating influence, is placed in pointed juxtaposition with a far more mordant address 'To Sickness'. In such ways the reader is constantly involved and reinvolved in the creation of moral perspectives in *The Forest*, a process of readjustment which leads inexorably 'To Heaven' (XV), a contemplation of ultimate truths which, in turn, cast their shadows back over preceding doubts and apparent certainties. The sequence has a unity which would barely be suspected on a first reading.

The Jonson I have been describing in these two collections is indeed a classicist — the whole concept of the *Epigrams* is developed from Martial; 'Come my Celia' is a careful adaptation of Catullus; 'Drink to me only' is a mosaic from the prose of Philostratus — and a moralist too. But he is primarily a poet, engaging us as only a poet can, emotionally and intellectually, in an examination of human standards and conduct. He is a challenging figure but not an inhuman or, I believe, an arrogant one. He finds a proper humility when he confronts his maker but even before his fellow men he cannot pretend to be all-knowing, all-perfect. Love catches out even him. It has been said that there is something improper in 'To Penshurst' (II) about Jonson's depiction (lines 67-8) of his own gargantuan appetites — 'Here no man tells my cups nor, standing by, / A waiter, doth my gluttony envy' — that it is out of place in that balanced, Edenic world. But I think this misses the point. It is precisely because Jonson is and (in his own way) admits to being so fallible that he is so passionately concerned about truth and standards in human life. Human nature being what it is (and Jonson at his best is not afraid to include himself), it may be that we will find no lasting solutions to any of these questions, this side of the grave. But Jonson is determined to keep reminding us that the questions exist, and that they matter.

A note on the text and punctuation

Epigrams and *The Forest* present no serious textual problems. Jonson published both in the 1616 Folio of his *Works*, a volume which he himself saw through the press with what, by the standards of the day, was unusual care. I follow that text throughout this edition, making only obvious corrections and elementary modernizations. The only significant exception is in *The Forest*, XII, 'Epistle to Elizabeth, Countess of Rutland'; in the Folio, Jonson abandons the poem at line 93, after 'Who wheresoe'er he be', presumably because the marriage (to the 'brave friend', the Earl of Rutland) was not consummated. The ending is supplied from manuscript copies.

Jonson was meticulous about his punctuation, the first significant English author so to be. The principles he followed are not those that were generally adopted later, and his use of commas and semi-colons, for example, is much heavier than our own. But Jonson's punctuation is often the key to his sense, as he points out himself in mocking Groom Idiot (*Epigrams*, LVIII): 'And so my sharpness thou no less disjoints, / Than thou didst late my sense, losing my points.' 'Points' here means both punctuation and subject-matter. For this reason I have disturbed Jonson's 'points' as little as possible, making changes only where a modern reader might be positively misled. It is useful to bear in mind that Jonson usually punctuates for the speaking voice, pointing up balanced phrases, cadences, antitheses, pauses — and so nuances, ambiguities; many apparent difficulties and irregularities in his verse disappear (while many subtleties emerge) when they are *spoken* as he directed. This is why I have also reproduced Jonson's consistent practice of eliding unstressed past participles ('look'd', 'nam'd', etc), which is a constant reminder of the fact that his poetry has, for all its reference to classical forms and themes, an energy and directness which is firmly rooted in colloquial, idiomatic English.

A note on the Notes

The assumption behind this edition is that Jonson's poems are still living works; they do not require a mass of annotation to make them intelligible. Inevitably, however, some local allusions and mythological references have lost their force down the ages, and some words have faded from the language or changed in meaning. Where this might pose a serious threat to the modern reader's enjoyment or understanding of the poetry, I have included a brief note. But I have not attempted to explain the more accessible mythological allusions or to offer biographical details of the people mentioned and addressed in his poems; in most cases, the poems themselves supply all the *essential* information if we read them closely enough. Anyone who feels the need for more information on any of these topics, or on Jonson's extensive use of classical sources, should consult the notes in the editions by Donaldson or Parfitt, cited in the Bibliography.

Select bibliography

The standard edition of Jonson's works is C.H. Herford, Percy and Evelyn Simpson, eds., *Ben Jonson*, 11 vols., Clarendon Press, 1925-52.

The Scolar Press published a facsimile of the 1616 First Folio in 1976.

Three recent editions of Jonson's complete non-dramatic verse are:

G.B. Johnston, ed., *Poems of Ben Jonson* (Muses Library), Routledge & Kegan Paul, 1954.

I. Donaldson, ed., *Ben Jonson: poems* (Oxford Standard Authors), Oxford University Press, 1975.

G.A.E. Parfitt, ed., *Ben Jonson: complete poems* (Penguin English Poets), Penguin Books, 1975. (This edition usefully also includes texts of *Conversations with Drummond* and *Timber: or Discoveries*).

Books of criticism on Jonson's poetry:

G.B. Johnston, *Ben Jonson: poet*, Columbia University Press, 1945.

W. Trimpi, *Ben Jonson's Poems*, Stanford University Press, 1962.

J.G. Nichols, *The Poetry of Ben Jonson*, Routledge & Kegan Paul, 1969.

Other relevant books:

J.A. Barish, ed., *Ben Jonson: a collection of critical essays*, Prentice-Hall, 1963.

W.R. Keast, ed., *Seventeenth Century English Poetry*, Oxford University Press, 1962.

G.A.E. Parfitt, *Ben Jonson: public poet and private man*, Dent, 1976.

Epigrams

*To the great example of Honour and Virtue, the most noble William,
Earl of Pembroke, Lord Chamberlain, etc*

*My lord. While you cannot change your merit, I dare not change
your title: it was that made it, and not I. Under which name, I here
offer to your lordship the ripest of my studies, my* Epigrams; *which,
though they carry danger in the sound, do not therefore seek your
shelter: for, when I made them, I had nothing in my conscience, to
expressing of which I did need a cipher. But, if I be fallen into those
times, wherein, for the likeness of vice, and facts, everyone thinks
another's ill deeds objected to him; and that in their ignorant and
guilty mouths, the common voice is (for their security) 'Beware the
poet', confessing, therein, so much love to their diseases, as they
would rather make a party for them, than be either rid, or told of
them: I must expect, at your lo[rdship's] hand, the protection of
truth, and liberty, while you are constant to your own goodness. In
thanks whereof, I return you the honour of leading forth so many
good, and great names (as my verses mention on the better part) to
their remembrance with posterity. Amongst whom, if I have praised,
unfortunately, anyone, that doth not deserve; or, if all answer not,
in all numbers, the pictures I have made of them: I hope it will be
forgiven me, that they are no ill pieces, though they be not like the
persons. But I foresee a nearer fate to my book, than this: that the
vices therein will be owned before the virtues (though, there, I have
avoided all particulars, as I have done names) and that some will be
so ready to discredit me, as they will have the impudence to belie
themselves. For, if I meant them not, it is so. Nor, can I hope
otherwise. For, why should they remit anything of their riot, their
pride, their self-love, and other inherent graces, to consider truth or
virtue; but, with the trade of the world, lend their long ears against
men they love not: and hold their dear mountebank, or jester, in far
better condition, than all study, or studiers of humanity? For such, I
would rather know them by their vizards, still, than they should
publish their faces, at their peril, in my theatre, where Cato, if he
lived, might enter without scandal.*

*Your lo[rdship's] most faithful honourer,
Ben. Jonson*

I *To the Reader*

Pray thee, take care, that tak'st my book in hand,
To read it well: that is, to understand.

II *To My Book*

It will be look'd for, book, when some but see
    Thy title, *Epigrams*, and nam'd of me,
Thou should'st be bold, licentious, full of gall,
    Wormwood, and sulphur, sharp, and tooth'd withal;
Become a petulant thing, hurl ink, and wit,
    As mad-men stones: not caring whom they hit.
Deceive their malice, who could wish it so.
    And by thy wiser temper, let men know
Thou art not covetous of least self-fame,
    Made from the hazard of another's shame: 10
Much less with lewd, profane, and beastly phrase,
    To catch the world's loose laughter, or vain gaze.
He that departs with his own honesty
    For vulgar praise, doth it too dearly buy.

III *To My Bookseller*

Thou, that mak'st gain thy end, and wisely well,
    Call'st a book good, or bad, as it doth sell,
Use mine so, too: I give thee leave. But crave
    For the luck's sake, it thus much favour have:
To lie upon thy stall, till it be sought;
    Not offer'd, as it made suit to be bought;
Nor have my title-leaf on posts, or walls,
    Or in cleft-sticks, advanced to make calls
For termers, or some clerk-like serving-man,
    Who scarce can spell the hard name: whose knight less can. 10

29

If, without these vile arts, it will not sell,
    Send it to Bucklersbury, there 'twill well.

IV   *To King James*

How, best of kings, dost thou a sceptre bear!
    How, best of poets, dost thou laurel wear!
But two things, rare, the Fates had in their store,
    And gave thee both, to show they could no more.
For such a poet, while thy days were green,
    Thou wert, as chief of them are said t'have been.
And such a prince thou art, we daily see,
    As chief of those still promise they will be.
Whom should my muse then fly to, but the best
    Of kings for grace; of poets for my test?

V   *On the Union*

When was there contract better driven by Fate?
    Or celebrated with more truth of state?
The world the temple was, the priest a king,
    The spoused pair two realms, the sea the ring.

VI   *To Alchemists*

If all you boast of your great art be true;
    Sure, willing poverty lives most in you.

VII   *On the New Hot-Houses*

Where lately harbour'd many a famous whore,
    A purging bill, now fix'd upon the door,

30

Tells you it is a hothouse: so it may,
    And still be a whore-house. They're *synonima*.

VIII   *On a Robbery*

Ridway robb'd Duncote of three hundred pound,
    Ridway was ta'en, arraign'd, condemn'd to die;
But, for this money was a courtier found,
    Begg'd Ridway's pardon: Duncote, now, doth cry;
Robb'd both of money, and the law's relief,
    The courtier is become the greater thief.

IX   *To All, To Whom I Write*

May none, whose scattered names honour my book,
    For strict degrees of rank, or title look:
'Tis 'gainst the manners of an epigram:
    And, I a poet here, no herald am.

X   *To My Lord Ignorant*

Thou call'st me poet, as a term of shame:
    But I have my revenge made, in thy name.

XI   *On Something, that Walks Somewhere*

At court I met it, in clothes brave enough,
    To be a courtier; and looks grave enough,
To seem a statesman: as I near it came,
    It made me a great face, I asked the name.
A lord, it cried, buried in flesh, and blood,
    And such from whom let no man hope least good,

31

For I will do none: and as little ill,
  For I will dare none. Good Lord, walk dead still.

Shift, here, in town, not meanest among squires,
  That haunt Pikthatch, Marshlambeth and Whitefriars,
Keeps himself, with half a man, and defrays
  The charge of that state, with this charm, god pays.
By that one spell he lives, eats, drinks, arrays
  Himself: his whole revenue is, god pays.
The quarter-day is come; the hostess says,
  She must have money: he returns, god pays.
The tailor brings a suit home; he it 'ssays,
  Looks o'er the bill, likes it: and says, god pays.   10
He steals to ordinaries; there he plays
  At dice his borrow'd money: which, god pays.
Then takes up fresh commodity, for days;
  Signs to new bond, forfeits: and cries, god pays.
That lost, he keeps his chamber, reads essays,
  Takes physic, tears the papers: still god pays.
Or else by water goes, and so to plays;
  Calls for his stool, adorns the stage: god pays.
To every cause he meets, this voice he brays:
  His only answer is to all, god pays.   20
Not his poor cockatrice but he betrays
  Thus: and for his lechery, scores, god pays.
But see! The old bawd hath served him in his trim,
  Lent him a pocky whore. She hath paid him.

When men a dangerous disease did 'scape,
  Of old, they gave a cock to Aesculape;

Let me give two: that doubly am got free,
From my disease's danger, and from thee.

XIV   *To William Camden*

Camden, most reverend head, to whom I owe
    All that I am in arts, all that I know,
(How nothing's that?) to whom my country owes
    The great renown, and name wherewith she goes.
Than thee the age sees not that thing more grave,
    More high, more holy, that she more would crave.
What name, what skill, what faith hast thou in things!
    What sight in searching the most antique springs!
What weight, and what authority, in thy speech!
    Man scarce can make that doubt, but thou canst teach.   10
Pardon free truth, and let thy modesty,
    Which conquers all, be once overcome by thee.
Many of thine this better could, than I,
    But for their powers, accept my piety.

XV   *On Court-Worm*

All men are worms: but this no man. In silk
    'Twas brought to court first wrapp'd, and white as milk;
Where, afterwards, it grew a butterfly:
    Which was a caterpillar. So 'twill die.

XVI   *To Brain-Hardy*

Hardy, thy brain is valiant, 'tis confess'd,
    Thou more; that with it every day, dar'st jest
Thyself into fresh brawls: when, call'd upon,
    Scarce thy week's swearing brings thee off, of one.

So, in short time, th'art in arrearage grown
    Some hundred quarrels, yet dost thou fight none;
Nor need'st thou: for those few, by oath releas'd,
    Make good what thou dar'st do in all the rest.
Keep thyself there, and think thy valour right,
    He that dares damn himself, dares more than fight.

XVII   *To the Learned Critic*

May others fear, fly, and traduce thy name,
    As guilty men do magistrates: glad I,
That wish my poems a legitimate fame,
    Charge them, for crown, to thy sole censure high.
And, but a sprig of bays given by thee,
    Shall outlive garlands, stol'n from the chaste tree.

XVIII   *To My Mere English Censurer*

To thee, my way in epigrams seems new,
    When both it is the old way, and the true.
Thou say'st, that cannot be: for thou hast seen
    Davies, and Weever, and the best have been,
And mine come nothing like. I hope so. Yet,
    As theirs did with thee, mine might credit get:
If thou'ld'st but use thy faith, as thou didst then,
    When thou wert wont t'admire, not censure men.
Prithee believe still, and not judge so fast,
    Thy faith is all the knowledge that thou hast.

XIX   *On Sir Cod the Perfumed*

That Cod can get no widow, yet a knight,
    I scent the cause: he woos with an ill sprite.

34

XX *To the Same Sir Cod*

Th'expense in odours is a most vain sin,
    Except thou could'st, Sir Cod, wear them within.

XXI *On Reformed Gamester*

Lord, how is gamester chang'd! His hair close cut!
    His neck fenc'd round with ruff! His eyes half shut!
His clothes two fashions off, and poor! His sword
    Forbid' his side! And nothing, but the Word
Quick in his lips! Who hath this wonder wrought?
    The late ta'en bastinado. So I thought.
What several ways men to their calling have!
    The body's stripes, I see, the soul may save.

XXII *On My First Daughter*

Here lies to each her parents' ruth,
Mary, the daughter of their youth:
Yet, all heaven's gifts, being heaven's due,
It makes the father, less to rue.
At six months' end, she parted hence
With safety of her innocence;
Whose soul heaven's queen, (whose name she bears)
In comfort of her mother's tears,
Hath placed amongst her virgin train:
Where, while that sever'd doth remain,   10
This grave partakes the fleshly birth.
Which cover lightly, gentle earth.

XXIII   *To John Donne*

Donne, the delight of Phoebus, and each muse,
    Who, to thy one, all other brains refuse;
Whose every work, of thy most early wit,
    Came forth example, and remains so, yet:
Longer a-knowing, than most wits do live.
    And which no affection praise enough can give!
To it, thy language, letters, arts, best life,
    Which might with half mankind maintain a strife.
All which I meant to praise, and, yet, I would;
    But leave, because I cannot as I should!

XXIV   *To the Parliament*

There's reason good, that you good laws should make:
    Men's manners ne'er were viler, for your sake.

XXV   *On Sir Voluptuous Beast*

While Beast instructs his fair, and innocent wife,
    In the past pleasures of his sensual life,
Telling the motions of each petticoat,
    And how his Ganymede moved, and how his goat,
And now, her (hourly) her own cucqueen makes,
    In varied shapes, which for his lust she takes:
What doth he else, but say, leave to be chaste,
    Just wife, and, to change me, make woman's haste.

XXVI   *On the Same Beast*

Than his chaste wife, though Beast now know no more,
    He adulters still: his thoughts lie with a whore.

XXVII   *On Sir John Roe*

In place of scutcheons, that should deck thy hearse,
Take better ornaments, my tears, and verse.
    If any sword could save from Fates, Roe's could;
    If any muse outlive their spite, his can;
    If any friend's tears could restore, his would;
    If any pious life e'er lifted man
To heaven, his hath: O happy state! wherein
We, sad for him, may glory, and not sin.

XXVIII   *On Don Surly*

Don Surly, to aspire the glorious name
    Of a great man, and to be thought the same,
Makes serious use of all great trade he knows.
    He speaks to men with a rhinocerote's nose,
Which he thinks great; and so reads verses, too:
    And, that is done, as he saw great men do.
H'has tympanies of business, in his face,
    And can forget men's names, with a great grace.
He will both argue, and discourse in oaths,
    Both which are great. And laugh at ill-made clothes;   10
That's greater, yet: to cry his own up neat.
    He doth, at meals, alone, his pheasant eat,
Which is main greatness. And, at his still board,
    He drinks to no man: that's, too, like a lord.
He keeps another's wife, which is a spice
    Of solemn greatness. And he dares, at dice,
Blaspheme God, greatly. Or some poor hind beat,
    That breathes in his dog's way: and this is great.
Nay more, for greatness' sake, he will be one
    May hear my *Epigrams*, but like of none.   20
Surly, use other arts, these only can
    Style thee a most great fool, but no great man.

37

XXIX   *To Sir Annual Tilter*

Tilter, the most may admire thee, though not I:
    And thou, right guiltless, mayst plead to it, why?
For thy late sharp device. I say 'tis fit
    All brains, at times of triumph, should run wit.
For then, our water-conduits do run wine;
    But that's put in, thou'lt say. Why, so is thine.

XXX   *To Person Guilty*

Guilty, be wise; and though thou know'st the crimes
    Be thine, I tax, yet do not own my rhymes:
'Twere madness in thee, to betray thy fame,
    And person to the world; ere I thy name.

XXXI   *On Bank the Usurer*

Bank feels no lameness of his knotty gout,
    His monies travel for him, in and out:
And though the soundest legs go every day,
    He toils to be at hell, as soon as they.

XXXII   *On Sir John Roe*

What two brave perils of the private sword
    Could not effect, not all the furies do,
That self-divided Belgia did afford;
    What not the envy of the seas reached to,
The cold of Moscow, and fat Irish air,
    His often change of clime (though not of mind)
What could not work; at home in his repair
    Was his blest state, but our hard lot to find.

38

Which shows, wherever death doth please t'appear,
    Seas, serenes, swords, shot, sickness, all are there.

XXXIII   *To the Same*

I'll not offend thee with a vain tear more,
    Glad-mention'd Roe: thou art but gone before,
Whither the world must follow. And I, now,
    Breathe to expect my when, and make my how.
Which if most gracious heaven grant like thine,
    Who wets my grave, can be no friend of mine.

XXXIV   *Of Death*

He that fears death, or mourns it, in the just,
    Shows of the resurrection little trust.

XXXV   *To King James*

Who would not be thy subject, James, t'obey
    A prince, that rules by example, more than sway?
Whose manners draw, more than thy powers constrain.
    And in this short time of thy happiest reign,
Hast purg'd thy realms, as we have now no cause
    Left us of fear, but first our crimes, then laws.
Like aids 'gainst treasons who hath found before?
    And than, in them, how could we know God more?
First thou preserved wert, our king to be,
    And since, the whole land was preserv'd for thee.

XXXVI   *To the Ghost of Martial*

Martial, thou gav'st far nobler epigrams
   To thy Domitian, than I can my James:
But in my royal subject I pass thee,
   Thou flattered'st thine, mine cannot flatter'd be.

XXXVII   *On Chev'ril the Lawyer*

No cause, nor client fat, will Chev'ril leese,
   But as they come, on both sides he takes fees,
And pleaseth both. For while he melts his grease
   For this: that wins, for whom he holds his peace.

XXXVIII   *To Person Guilty*

Guilty, because I bad you late be wise,
   And to conceal your ulcers, did advise,
You laugh when you are touch'd, and long before
   Any man else, you clap your hands, and roar,
And cry good! good! This quite perverts my sense,
   And lies so far from wit, 'tis impudence.
Believe it, Guilty, if you lose your shame,
   I'll lose my modesty, and tell your name.

XXXIX   *On Old Colt*

For all night sins, with others' wives, unknown,
   Colt, now, doth daily penance in his own.

XL   *On Margaret Ratcliffe*

M   arble, weep, for thou dost cover
A   dead beauty underneath thee,
R   ich, as nature could bequeath thee:
G   rant then, no rude hand remove her.
A   ll the gazers on the skies
R   ead not in fair heaven's story,
E   xpresser truth, or truer glory,
T   han they might in her bright eyes.
R   are, as wonder, was her wit;
A   nd like nectar ever flowing: 10
T   ill time, strong by her bestowing,
C   onquered hath both life and it.
L   ife, whose grief was out of fashion,
I   n these times. Few so have ru'd
F   ate, in a brother. To conclude,
F   or wit, feature, and true passion,
E   arth, thou hast not such another.

XLI   *On Gypsy*

Gypsy, new bawd, is turn'd phsyician,
    And gets more gold, than all the college can:
Such her quaint practice is, so it allures,
    For what she gave, a whore; a bawd, she cures.

XLII   *On Giles and Joan*

Who says that Giles and Joan at discord be?
    Th'observing neighbours no such mood can see.
Indeed, poor Giles repents he married ever.
    But that his Joan doth too. And Giles would never,

By his free will, be in Joan's company.
  No more would Joan he should. Giles riseth early,
And having got him out of doors is glad.
  The like is Joan. But turning home, is sad.
And so is Joan. Oft-times, when Giles doth find
  Harsh sights at home, Giles wisheth he were blind.   10
All this doth Joan. Or that his long-yarn'd life
  Were quite out-spun. The like wish hath his wife.
The children, that he keeps, Giles swears are none
  Of his begetting. And so swears his Joan.
In all affections she concurreth still.
  If, now, with man and wife, to will, and nill
The self-same things, a note of concord be:
  I know no couple better can agree!

XLIII   *To Robert, Earl of Salisbury*

What need hast thou of me? Or of my muse?
  Whose actions so themselves do celebrate?
Which should thy country's love to speak refuse,
  Her foes enough would fame thee in their hate.
'Tofore, great men were glad of poets: now,
  I, not the worst, am covetous of thee.
Yet dare not, to my thought, least hope allow.
  Of adding to thy fame; thine may to me,
When in my book, men read but Cecil's name,
  And what I write thereof find far, and free   10
From servile flattery (common poets' shame)
  As thou stand'st clear of the necessity.

XLIV   *On Chuff, Banks the Usurer's Kinsman*

Chuff, lately rich in name, in chattels, goods,
  And rich in issue to inherit all,

42

Ere blacks were bought for his own funeral,
Saw all his race approach the blacker floods:
    He meant they thither should make swift repair,
    When he made him executor, might be heir.

XLV   *On My First Son*

Farewell, thou child of my right hand, and joy;
    My sin was too much hope of thee, lov'd boy,
Seven years thou wert lent to me, and I thee pay,
    Exacted by thy fate, on the just day.
O, could I lose all father, now. For why
    Will man lament the state he should envy?
To have so soon 'scap'd world's, and flesh's rage,
    And if no other misery, yet age?
Rest in soft peace, and, ask'd, say here doth lie
    Ben. Jonson his best piece of poetry.
For whose sake, henceforth, all his vows be such,
    As what he loves may never like too much.

XLVI   *To Sir Luckless Woo-All*

Is this the sir, who, some waste wife to win,
    A knighthood bought, to go a-wooing in?
'Tis Luckless he, that took up one on band
    To pay at's day of marriage. By my hand
The knight-wright's cheated then: he'll never pay.
    Yes, now he wears his knighthood every day.

XLVII   *To the Same*

Sir Luckless, troth, for luck's sake pass by one:
    He that woos every widow, will get none.

43

XLVIII   *On Mongrel Esquire*

His bought arms Mong' not lik'd; for his first day
   Of bearing them in field, he threw'em away:
And hath no honour lost, our duellists say.

XLIX   *To Playwright*

Playwright me reads, and still my verses damns,
   He says, I want the tongue of epigrams;
I have no salt: no bawdry he doth mean.
   For witty, in his language, is obscene.
Playwright, I loath to have thy manners known
   In my chaste book: profess them in thine own.

L   *To Sir Cod*

Leave Cod, tobacco-like, burnt gums to take,
   Or fumy clysters, thy moist lungs to bake:
Arsenic would thee fit for society make.

LI   *To King James*

*Upon the happy false rumour of his death, the two and twentieth
day of March, 1607*

That we thy loss might know, and thou our love,
   Great heaven did well, to give ill fame free wing;
Which though it did but panic terror prove,
   And far beneath least pause of such a king,
Yet give thy jealous subjects leave to doubt:
   Who this thy 'scape from rumour gratulate,

No less than if from peril; and devout,
  Do beg thy care unto thy after-state.
For we, that have our eyes still in our ears,
  Look not upon thy dangers, but our fears.

LII *To Censorious Courtling*

Courtling, I rather thou should'st utterly
  Dispraise my work, than praise it frostily:
When I am read, thou feign'st a weak applause,
  As if thou wert my friend, but lack'st a cause.
This but thy judgement fools: the other way
  Would both thy folly, and thy spite betray.

LIII *To Old-End Gatherer*

Long-gathering Old-End, I did fear thee wise,
  When having pill'd a book, which no man buys,
Thou wert content the author's name to lose:
  But when (in place) thou didst the patron's choose,
It was as if thou printed hadst an oath,
  To give the world assurance thou wert both;
And that, as puritans at baptism do,
  Thou art the father, and the witness too.
For, but thyself, where, out of motley, 's he
  Could save that line to dedicate to thee?   10

LIV *On Chev'ril*

Chev'ril cries out, my verses libels are;
  And threatens the Star Chamber, and the bar:
What are thy petulant pleadings, Chev'ril, then,
  That quit'st the cause so oft, and rail'st at men?

LV   *To Francis Beaumont*

How I do love thee Beaumont, and thy muse,
   That unto me dost such religion use!
How I do fear myself, that am not worth
   The least indulgent thought thy pen drops forth!
At once thou mak'st me happy, and unmak'st;
   And giving largely to me, more thou tak'st.
What fate is mine, that so itself bereaves?
   What art is thine, that so thy friend deceives?
When even there, where most thou praisest me,
   For writing better, I must envy thee.

LVI   *On Poet-Ape*

Poor Poet-Ape, that would be thought our chief,
   Whose works are e'en the frippery of wit,
From brocage is become so bold a thief,
   As we, the robb'd, leave rage, and pity it.
At first he made low shifts, would pick and glean,
   Buy the reversion of old plays; now grown
To a little wealth, and credit in the scene,
   He takes up all, makes each man's wit his own.
And, told of this, he slights it. Tut, such crimes
   The sluggish gaping auditor devours;   10
He marks not whose 'twas first: and after-times
   May judge it to be his, as well as ours.
Fool, as if half eyes will not know a fleece
   From locks of wool, or shreds from the whole piece!

LVII   *On Bawds, and Usurers*

If, as their ends, their fruits were so, the same,
   Bawdry, and usury were one kind of game.

46

LV   *To Groom Idiot*

Idiot, last night, I pray'd thee but forbear
   To read my verses; now I must to hear:
For offering, with thy smiles, my wit to grace,
   Thy ignorance still laughs in the wrong place.
And so my sharpness thou no less disjoints,
   Than thou didst late my sense, losing my points.
So have I seen at Christmas sports one lost,
   And, hood-wink'd, for a man, embrace a post.

LIX   *On Spies*

Spies, you are lights in state, but of base stuff,
   Who, when you have burnt yourselves down to the snuff,
Stink, and are thrown away. End fair enough.

LX   *To William, Lord Mounteagle*

Lo, what my country should have done (have rais'd
   An obelisk, or column to thy name,
Or, if she would but modestly have prais'd
   Thy fact, in brass or marble writ the same)
I, that am glad of thy great chance, here do!
   And proud, my work shall outlast common deeds,
Durst think it great, and worthy wonder too,
   But thine, for which I do it, so much exceeds!
My country's parents I have many known;
   But saver of my country thee alone.

LXI   *To Fool, or Knave*

Thy praise, or dispraise is to me alike,
   One doth not stroke me, nor the other strike.

LXII   *To Fine Lady Would-Be*

Fine Madam Would-Be, wherefore should you fear,
   That love to make so well, a child to bear?
The world reputes you barren: but I know
   Your 'pothecary, and his drug says no.
Is it the pain affrights? That's soon forgot.
   Or your complexion's loss? You have a pot,
That can restore that. Will it hurt your feature?
   To make amends, you're thought a wholesome creature.
What should the cause be? Oh, you live at court:
   And there's both loss of time, and loss of sport   10
In a great belly. Write, then on thy womb,
   Of the not born, yet buried, here's the tomb.

LXIII   *To Robert, Earl of Salisbury*

Who can consider thy right courses run,
   With what thy virtue on the times hath won,
And not thy fortune; who can clearly see
   The judgement of the king so shine in thee;
And that thou seek'st reward of thy each act,
   Not from the public voice, but private fact;
Who can behold all envy so declin'd
   By constant suffering of thy equal mind;
And can to these be silent, Salisbury,
   Without his, thine, and all times' injury?   10
Curst be his muse, that could lie dumb, or hid
   To so true worth, though thou thyself forbid.

LXIV   *To the Same*
     (*Upon the Accession of the Treasurership to him*)

Not glad, like those that have new hopes, or suits,
   With thy new place, bring I these early fruits

48

Of love, and what the golden age did hold
  A treasure, art: contemn'd in th'age of gold.
Nor glad as those, that old dependants be,
  To see thy father's rights new laid on thee.
Nor glad for fashion. Nor to show a fit
  Of flattery to thy titles. Nor of wit.
But I am glad to see that time survive,
  Where merit is not sepulcher'd alive.   10
Where good men's virtues them to honours bring,
  And not to dangers. When so wise a king
Contends to have worth enjoy, from his regard,
  As her own conscience, still, the same reward.
These (noblest Cecil) labour'd in my thought,
  Wherein what wonder see thy name hath wrought!
That whilst I meant but thine to gratulate,
  I have sung the greater fortunes of our state.

LXV   *To My Muse*

Away, and leave me, thou thing most abhorr'd
  That hast betray'd me to a worthless lord;
Made me commit most fierce idolatry
  To a great image through thy luxury.
Be thy next master's more unlucky muse,
  And, as thou hast mine, his hours, and youth abuse.
Get him the time's long grudge, the court's ill will;
  And, reconcil'd, keep him suspected still.
Make him lose all his friends; and, which is worse,
  Almost all ways, to any better course.   10
With me thou leav'st an happier muse than thee,
  And which thou brought'st me, welcome poverty.
She shall instruct my after-thoughts to write
  Things manly, and not smelling parasite.
But I repent me: stay. Whoe'er is rais'd,
  For worth he has not, he is tax'd, not prais'd.

LXVI   *To Sir Henry Cary*

That neither fame, nor love might wanting be
  To greatness, Cary, I sing that, and thee.
Whose house, if it no other honour had,
  In only thee, might be both great, and glad.
Who, to upbraid the sloth of this our time,
  Durst valour make, almost, but not a crime.
Which deed I know not, whether were more high,
  Or thou more happy, it to justify
Against thy fortune: when no foe, that day,
  Could conquer thee, but chance, who did betray.   10
Love thy great loss, which a renown hath won,
  To live when Broeck not stands, nor Ruhr doth run.
Love honours, which of best example be,
  When they cost dearest, and are done most free,
Though every fortitude deserves applause;
  It may be much, or little, in the cause.
He's valiant, that dares fight, and not for pay;
  That virtuous is, when the reward's away.

LXVII   *To Thomas, Earl of Suffolk*

Since man have left to do praise-worthy things,
  Most think all praises flattery. But truth brings
That sound, and that authority with her name,
  As, to be rais'd by her, is only fame.
Stand high, then, Howard, high in eyes of men,
  High in thy blood, thy place, but highest then,
When, in men's wishes, so thy virtues wrought,
  As all thy honours were by them first sought:
And thou design'd to be the same thou art,
  Before thou wert it, in each good man's heart.   10
Which, by no less confirm'd, than thy king's choice,
  Proves, that is God's, which was the people's voice.

LXVIII   *On Playwright*

Playwright convict of public wrongs to men,
  Takes private beatings, and begins again.
Two kinds of valour he doth show at once;
  Active in's brain, and passive in his bones.

LXIX   *To Pertinax Cob*

Cob, thou nor soldier, thief, nor fencer art,
  Yet by thy weapon liv'st! Th'hast one good part.

LXX   *To William Roe*

When Nature bids us leave to live, 'tis late
  Then to begin, my Roe: he makes a state
In life, that can employ it; and takes hold
  On the true causes, ere they grow too old.
Delay is bad, doubt worse, depending worst;
  Each best day of our life escapes us, first.
Then, since we (more than many) these truths know:
  Though life be short, let us not make it so.

LXXI   *On Court-Parrot*

To pluck down mine, Poll sets up new wits still,
  Still, 'tis his luck to praise me 'gainst his will.

LXXII   *To Courtling*

I grieve not, Courtling, thou art started up
  A chamber-critic, and dost dine and sup

At madam's table, where thou mak'st all wit
    Go high, or low, as thou wilt value it.
'Tis not thy judgement breeds the prejudice,
    Thy person only, Courtling, is the vice.

LXIII   *To Fine Grand*

What is't, fine Grand, makes thee my friendship fly,
    Or take an epigram so fearfully:
As 'twere a challenge, or a borrower's letter?
    The world must know your greatness is my debtor.
In primis, Grand, you owe me for a jest;
    I lent you, on mere acquaintance, at a feast.
Item, a tale or two, some fortnight after,
    That yet maintains you, and your house in laughter.
Item, the Babylonian song you sing;
    Item, a fair Greek posy for a ring: 10
With which a learned madam you belie.
    Item, a charm surrounding fearfully,
Your *partie-per-pale* picture, one half drawn
    In solemn cypress, the other cobweb lawn.
Item, a gulling imprese for you, at tilt.
    Item, your mistress' anagram, i'your hilt.
Item, your own, sew'd in your mistress' smock.
    Item, an epitaph on my lord's cock,
In most vile verses, and cost me more pain,
    Than had I made them good, to fit your vein.   20
Forty things more, dear Grand, which you know true,
    For which, or pay me quickly, or I'll pay you.

LXXIV   *To Thomas, Lord Chancellor*

Whilst thy weigh'd judgements, Egerton, I hear,
    And know thee, then, a judge, not of one year;

Whilst I behold thee live with purest hands;
  That no affection in thy voice commands;
That still th'art present to the better cause;
  And no less wise, than skilful in the laws;
Whilst thou art certain to thy words, once gone,
  As is thy conscience, which is always one:
The virgin, long-since fled from earth, I see,
  T'our times return'd, hath made her heaven in thee.   10

LXXV   *On Lip, the Teacher*

I cannot think there's that antipathy
  'Twixt puritans, and players, as some cry;
Though Lip, at Paul's, ran from his text away,
  T'inveigh 'gainst plays: what did he then but play?

LXXVI   *On Lucy, Countess of Bedford*

This morning, timely rapt with holy fire,
  I thought to form unto my zealous muse,
What kind of creature I could most desire,
  To honour, serve, and love; as poets use.
I meant to make her fair, and free, and wise,
  Of greatest blood, and yet more good than great;
I meant the day-star should not brighter rise,
  Nor lend like influence from his lucent seat.
I meant she should be courteous, facile, sweet,
  Hating that solemn vice of greatness, pride;   10
I meant each softest virtue, there should meet,
  Fit in that softer bosom to reside.
Only a learned, and a manly soul
  I purpos'd her; that should, with even powers,
The rock, the spindle, and the shears control
  Of destiny, and spin her own free hours.

Such when I meant to feign, and wish'd to see,
  My muse bad, *Bedford* write, and that was she.

LXXVII   *To One that Desired Me Not to Name Him*

Be safe, nor fear thyself so good a fame,
  That, any way, my book should speak thy name:
For, if thou shame, rank'd with my friends, to go,
  I'm more asham'd to have thee thought my foe.

LXXVIII   *To Hornet*

Hornet, thou hast thy wife dress'd, for the stall,
  To draw the custom: but herself gets all.

LXXIX   *To Elizabeth, Countess of Rutland*

That poets are far rarer births than kings,
  Your noblest father prov'd: like whom, before,
Or then, or since, about our muses' springs,
  Came not that soul exhausted so their store.
Hence was it, that the destinies decreed
  (Save that most masculine issue of his brain)
No male unto him: who could so exceed
  Nature, they thought, in all, that he would feign.
At which, she happily displeas'd, made you:
  On whom, if he were living now, to look,   10
He should those rare, and absolute numbers view,
  As he would burn, or better far his book.

LXXX *Of Life, and Death*

The ports of death are sins; of life, good deeds:
   Through which, our merit leads us to our meeds.
How wilful blind is he then, that would stray,
   And hath it, in his powers, to make his way!
This world death's region is, the other life's:
   And here, it should be one of our first strifes,
So to front death, as men might judge us past it.
   For good men but see death, the wicked taste it.

LXXXI *To Prowl the Plagiary*

Forbear to tempt me, Prowl, I will not show
   A line unto thee, till the world it know;
Or that I have by two good sufficient men,
   To be the wealthy witness of my pen:
For all thou hear'st, thou swear'st thyself didst do.
   Thy wit lives by it, Prowl, and belly too.
Which, if thou leave not soon (though I am loathe)
   I must a libel make, and cozen both.

LXXXII *On Cashiered Capt(ain) Surly*

Surly's old whore in her new silks doth swim:
   He cast, yet keeps her well! No, she keeps him.

LXXXIII *To a Friend*

To put out the word, whore, thou dost me woo,
   Throughout my book. 'Troth put out woman too.

LXXXIV   *To Lucy, Countess of Bedford*

Madam, I told you late how I repented,
   I ask'd a lord a buck, and he denied me;
And, ere I could ask you, I was prevented:
   For your most noble offer had suppli'd me.
Straight went I home; and there most like a poet,
   I fancied to myself, what wine, what wit
I would have spent: how every muse should know it,
   And Phoebus' self should be at eating it.
O madam, if your grant did thus transfer me,
   Make it your gift. See whither that will bear me.   10

LXXXV   *To Sir Henry Goodyere*

Goodyere, I am glad, and grateful to report,
   Myself a witness of thy few days' sport:
Where I both learn'd, why wise men hawking follow,
   And why that bird was sacred to Apollo;
She doth instruct men by her gallant flight,
   That they to knowledge so should tower upright,
And never stoop, but to strike ignorance:
   Which if they miss, they yet should re-advance
To former height, and there in circle tarry,
   Till they be sure to make the fool their quarry.   10
Now, in whose pleasures I have this discerned,
   What would his serious actions me have learned?

LXXXVI   *To the Same*

When I would know thee Goodyere, my thought looks
   Upon thy well-made choice of friends, and books;
Then do I love thee, and behold thy ends
   In making thy friends books, and thy books friends:

56

Now, I must give thy life, and deed, the voice
   Attending such a study, such a choice.
Where, though't be love, that to thy praise doth move,
   It was a knowledge, that begat that love.

LXXXVII   *On Captain Hazard the Cheater*

Touch'd with the sin of false play, in his punk,
   Hazard a month forswore his; and grew drunk,
Each night, to drown his cares: but when the gain
   Of what she had wrought came in, and wak'd his brain,
Upon the account, hers grew the quicker trade.
   Since when, he's sober again, and all play's made.

LXXXVIII   *On English Monsieur*

Would you believe, when you this Monsieur see,
   That his whole body should speak French, not he?
That so much scarf of France, and hat, and feather,
   And shoe, and tie, and garter should come hither,
And land on one, whose face durst never be
   Toward the sea, farther than half-way tree?
That he, untravell'd, should be French so much,
   As Frenchmen in his company, should seem Dutch?
Or had his father, when he did him get,
   The French disease, with which he labours yet?   10
Or hung some Monsieur's picture on the wall,
   By which his dam conceiv'd him clothes and all?
Or is it some French statue? No: 't doth move,
   And stoop, and cringe. O then, it needs must prove
The new French tailor's motion, monthly made,
   Daily to turn in Paul's, and help the trade.

LXXXIX *To Edward Alleyn*

If Rome so great, and in her wisest age,
   Fear'd not to boast the glories of her stage,
As skilful Roscius, and grave Aesop, men,
   Yet crown'd with honours, as with riches, then;
Who had no less a trumpet of their name,
   Than Cicero, whose every breath was fame:
How can so great example die in me,
   That, Alleyn, I should pause to publish thee?
Who both their graces in thyself hast more
   Out-stripp'd, than they did all that went before: 10
And present worth in all dost so contract,
   As others speak, but only thou dost act.
Wear this renown. 'Tis just, that who did give
   So many poets life, by one should live.

XC   *On Mill, My Lady's Woman*

When Mill first came to court, the unprofiting fool,
   Unworthy such a mistress, such a school,
Was dull, and long, ere she would go to man:
   At last, ease, appetite, and example wan
The nicer thing to taste her lady's page;
   And, finding good security in his age,
Went on: and proving him still, day by day,
   Discern'd no difference of his years, or play.
Not though that hair grew brown, which once was amber,
   And he grown youth, was called to his lady's chamber.   10
Still Mill continu'd: nay, his face growing worse,
   And he remov'd to gent'man of the horse,
Mill was the same. Since, both his body and face
   Blown up; and he (too unwieldy for that place)
Hath got the steward's chair; he will not tarry
   Longer a day, but with his Mill will marry.

And it is hoped, that she, like Milo, wull
   First bearing him a calf, bear him a bull.

XCI   *To Sir Horace Vere*

Which of thy names I take, not only bears
   A Roman sound, but Roman virtue wears,
Illustrous Vere, or Horace; fit to be
   Sung by a Horace, or a muse as free;
Which thou art to thyself: whose fame was won
   In the eye of Europe, where thy deeds were done,
When on thy trumpet she did sound a blast,
   Whose relish to eternity shall last.
I leave thy acts, which should I prosecute
   Throughout, might flattery seem; and to be mute   10
To any one, were envy: which would live
   Against my grave, and time could not forgive.
I speak thy other graces, not less shown,
   Nor less in practice; but less marked, less known:
Humanity, and piety, which are
   As noble in great chiefs, as they are rare.
And best become the valiant man to wear,
   Who more should seek men's reverence, than fear.

XCII   *The New Cry*

Ere cherries ripe, and strawberries be gone,
   Unto the cries of London I'll add one;
Ripe statesmen, ripe: they grow in every street.
   At six and twenty, ripe. You shall them meet,
And have them yield no savour, but of state.
   Ripe are their ruffs, their cuffs, their beard, their gait,
And grave as ripe, like mellow as their faces,
   They know the states of Christendom, not the places:

Yet have they seen the maps, and bought them too,
  And understand them, as most chapmen do.   10
The councils, projects, practices they know,
  And what each prince doth for intelligence owe,
And unto whom: they are the almanacs
  For twelve years yet to come, what each state lacks.
They carry in their pockets Tacitus,
  And the gazetti, or *Gallo-Belgicus*:
And talk reserv'd, lock'd up, and full of fear,
  Nay, ask you, how the day goes, in your ear.
Keep a Star Chamber sentence close, twelve days:
  And whisper what a proclamation says.   20
They meet in sixes, and at every mart,
  Are sure to con the catalogue by heart;
Or, every day, some one at Rimee's looks,
  Or Bill's, and there he buys the names of books.
They all get Porta, for the sundry ways
  To write in cipher, and the several keys,
To ope the character. They have found the sleight
  With juice of lemons, onions, piss, to write.
To break up seals, and close them. And they know,
  If the States make peace, how it will go   30
With England. All forbidden books they get.
  And of the powder plot, they will talk yet.
At naming the French king, their heads they shake,
  And at the Pope, and Spain slight faces make.
Or 'gainst the bishops, for the Brethren, rail,
  Much like those Brethren; thinking to prevail
With ignorance on us, as they have done
  On them: and therefore do not only shun
Others more modest, but contemn us too,
  That know not so much state, wrong, as they do.   40

XCIII   *To Sir John Radcliffe*

How like a column, Radcliffe, left alone
 For the great mark of virtue, those being gone
Who did, alike with thee, thy house up-bear,
 Stand'st thou, to show the times what you all were!
Two bravely in the battle fell, and died,
 Upbraiding rebels' arms, and barbarous pride:
And two, that would have fallen as great, as they,
 The Belgic fever ravished away.
Thou, that art all their valour, all their spirit,
 And thine own goodness to increase thy merit,   10
Than whose I do not know a whiter soul,
 Nor could I, had I seen all Nature's roll,
Thou yet remain'st, unhurt in peace, or war,
 Though not unprov'd: which shows, thy fortunes are
Willing to expiate the fault in thee,
 Wherewith, against thy blood, they offenders be.

XCIV   *To Lucy, Countess of Bedford, with Mr Donne's Satires*

Lucy, you brightness of our sphere, who are
 Life of the muse's day, their morning star!
If works (not th'authors) their own grace should look,
 Whose poems would not wish to be you book?
But these, desir'd by you, the maker's ends
 Crown with their own. Rare poems ask rare friends.
Yet, satires, since the most of mankind be
 Their unavoided subject, fewest see:
For none e'er took that pleasure in sin's sense,
 But, when they heard it tax'd, took more offence.   10
They, then, that living where the matter is bred,
 Dare for these poems, yet, both ask, and read,
And like them too; must needfully, though few,
 Be of the best: and 'mongst those, best are you.

61

Lucy, you brightness of our sphere, who are
    The muses' evening, as their morning star.

XCV   *To Sir Henry Savile*

If, my religion safe, I durst embrace
    That stranger doctrine of Pythagoras,
I should believe, the soul of Tacitus
    In thee, most weighty Savile, lived to us:
So hast thou render'd him in all his bounds,
    And all his numbers, both of sense, and sounds.
But when I read that special piece, restor'd,
    Where Nero falls, and Galba is ador'd,
To thine own proper I ascribe then more;
    And gratulate the breach, I griev'd before: 10
Which Fate (it seems) caused in the history,
    Only to boast thy merit in supply.
O, would'st thou add like hand, to all the rest!
    Or, better work! were thy glad country bless'd,
To have her story woven in thy thread;
    Minerva's loom was never richer spread.
For who can master those great parts like thee,
    That liv'st from hope, from fear, from faction free;
That hast thy breast so clear of present crimes,
    Thou need'st not shrink at voice of after-times;   20
Whose knowledge claimeth at the helm to stand;
    But, wisely, thrusts not forth a forward hand,
No more than Sallust in the Roman state!
    As, then, his cause, his glory emulate.
Although to write be lesser than to do,
    It is the next deed, and a great one too.
We need a man that knows the several graces
    Of history, and how to apt their places;
Where brevity, where splendour, and where height,
    Where sweetness is requir'd, and where weight;   30

We need a man, can speak of the intents,
　　The councils, actions, orders, and events
Of state, and censure them: we need his pen
　　Can write these things, the causes, and the men.
But most we need his faith (and all have you)
　　That dares not write things false, nor hide things true.

XCVI　*To John Donne*

Who shall doubt, Donne, where I a poet be,
　　When I dare send my epigrams to thee?
That so alone canst judge, so alone dost make:
　　And, in thy censures, evenly, dost take
As free simplicity, to dis-avow,
　　As thou hast best authority, t'allow.
Read all I send: and if I find but one
　　Mark'd by thy hand, and with the better stone,
My title's seal'd. Those that for claps do write,
　　Let puisnees', porters', players' praise delight,　　　10
And, till they burst, their backs, like asses, load:
　　A man should seek great glory, and not broad.

XCVII　*On the New Motion*

See you yond' motion? Not the old fading,
　　Nor Captain Pod, nor yet the Eltham thing;
But one more rare, and in the case so new:
　　His cloak with orient velvet quite lin'd through,
His rosy ties and garters so o'er-blown,
　　By his each glorious parcel to be known!
He wont was to encounter me, aloud,
　　Where e'er he met me; now he's dumb, or proud.
Know you the cause? He has neither land, nor lease,
　　Nor bawdy stock, that travels for increase,　　　10

Nor office in the town, nor place in court,
   Nor 'bout the bears, nor noise to make lords sport.
He is no favourite's favourite, no dear trust
   Of any madams hath neadd squires, and must.
Nor did the King of Denmark him salute,
   When he was here. Nor hath he got a suit,
Since he was gone, more than the one he wears.
   Nor are the Queen's most honoured maids by th'ears
About his form. What then so swells each limb?
   Only his clothes have over-leaven'd him.   20

XCVIII   *To Sir Thomas Roe*

Thou hast begun well, Roe, which stand well too,
   And I know nothing more thou hast to do.
He that is round within himself, and straight,
   Need seek no other strength, no other height;
Fortune upon him breaks herself, if ill,
   And what would hurt his virtue makes it still.
That thou at once, then, nobly may'st defend
   With thine own course the judgement of thy friend,
Be always to thy gather'd self the same:
   And study conscience, more than thou wouldst fame.   10
Though both be good, the latter yet is worst,
   And ever is ill got without the first.

XCIX   *To the Same*

That thou hast kept thy love, increas'd thy will,
   Better'd thy trust to letters; that thy skill;
Hast taught thyself worthy thy pen to tread,
   And that to write things worthy to be read:

64

How much of great example wert thou, Roe,
    If time to facts, as unto men would owe?
But much of it now avails, what's done, of whom:
    The self-same deeds, as diversely they come,
From place, or fortune, are made high, or low,
    And even the praiser's judgement suffers so.   10
Well, though thy name less than our great ones' be,
    Thy fact is more: let truth encourage thee.

C   *On Playwright*

Playwright, by chance, hearing some toys I had writ,
    Cried to my face, they were the elixir of wit:
And I must now believe him: for, today,
    Five of my jests, then stolen, pass'd him a play.

CI   *Inviting a Friend to Supper*

Tonight, grave sir, both my poor house, and I
    Do equally desire your company:
Not that we think us worthy such a guest,
    But that your worth will dignify our feast,
With those that come; whose grace may make that seem
    Something, which, else, could hope for no esteem.
It is the fair acceptance, sir, creates
    The entertainment perfect: not the cates.
Yet shall you have, to rectify your palate,
    An olive, capers, or some better salad   10
Ush'ring the mutton; with a short-legg'd hen,
    If we can get her, full of eggs, and then,
Lemons, and wine for sauce: to these, a coney
    Is not to be despair'd of, for our money;
And, though fowl, now, be scarce, yet there are clerks,
    The sky not falling, think we may have larks.

65

I'll tell you of more, and lie, so you will come:
  Of partridge, pheasant, wood-cock, of which some
May yet be there; and godwit, if we can:
  Knat, rail, and ruff too. Howsoe'er, my man   20
Shall read a piece of Virgil, Tacitus,
  Livy, or of some better book to us,
Of which we'll speak our minds, amidst our meat;
  And I'll profess no verses to repeat:
To this, if aught appear, which I know not of,
  That will the pastry, not my paper, show of.
Digestive cheese, and fruit there sure will be;
  But that, which most doth take my muse, and me,
Is a pure cup of rich canary wine,
  Which is the Mermaid's, now, but shall be mine: 30
Of which had Horace, or Anacreon tasted,
  Their lives, as do their lines, till now had lasted.
Tobacco, nectar, or the Thespian spring,
  Are all but Luther's beer, to this I sing.
Of this we will sup free, but moderately,
  And we will have no Pooly, or Parrot by;
Nor shall our cups make any guilty men:
  But at our parting, we will be, as when
We innocently met. No simple word,
  That shall be utter'd at our mirthful board,   40
Shall make us sad next morning: or affright
  The liberty, that we'll enjoy tonight.

CII   *To William, Earl of Pembroke*

I do but name thee Pembroke, and I find
  It is an epigram, on all mankind;
Against the bad, but of, and to be good:
  Both which are ask'd, to have thee understood.
Nor could the age have miss'd thee in this strife
  Of vice, and virtue; wherein all great life

66

Almost, is exercis'd: and scarce one knows,
  To which, yet, of the sides himself he owes.
They follow virtue, for reward, today;
  Tomorrow vice, if she give better pay: 10
And are so good, and bad, just at a price,
  As nothing else discerns the virtue or vice.
But thou, whose noblesse keeps one stature still,
  And one true posture, though besieg'd with ill
Of what ambition, faction, pride, can raise;
  Whose life, even they, that envy it, must praise;
That art so reverenc'd, as thy coming in,
  But in the view, doth interrupt their sin;
Thou must draw more: and they, that hope to see
  The commonwealth still safe, must study thee.   20

CIII   *To Mary, Lady Wroth*

How well, fair crown of your fair sex, might he,
  That but the twilight of your sprite did see,
And noted for what flesh such souls were fram'd,
  Know you to be a Sidney, though un-nam'd?
And, being nam'd, how little doth that name
  Need any muse's praise to give it fame?
Which is, itself, the imprese of the great,
  And glory of them all, but to repeat!
Forgive me then, if mine but say you are
  A Sidney: but in that extend as far   10
As loudest praisers, who perhaps would find
  For every part a character assign'd.
My praise is plain, and wheresoe'er profess'd,
  Becomes none more than you, who need it least.

CIV   *To Susan, Countess of Montgomery*

Were they that nam'd you, prophets? Did they see,
  Even in the dew of grace, what you would be?
Or did our times require it, to behold
  A new Susanna, equal to that old?
Or, because some scarce think that story true,
  To make those faithful, did the Fates send you?
And to your scene lent no less dignity
  Of birth, of match, of form, of chastity?
Or, more than born for the comparison
  Of former age, or glory of our one,   10
Were you advanced, past those times, to be
  The light, and mark unto posterity?
Judge they, that can: here I have rais'd to show
  A picture, which the world for yours must know,
And like it too; if they look equally:
  If not, 'tis fit for you, some should envy.

CV   *To Mary, Lady Wroth*

Madam, had all antiquity been lost,
  All history seal'd up, and fables cross'd;
That we had left us, nor by time, nor place,
  Least mention of a nymph, a muse, a grace,
But even their names were to be made anew,
  Who could not but create them all, from you?
He that but saw you wear the wheaten hat,
  Would call you more than Ceres, if not that:
And, dress'd in shepherd's 'tire, who would not say:
  You were the bright Oenone, Flora, or May?   10
If dancing, all would cry the Idalian Queen,
  Were leading forth the graces on the green:
And, armed to the chase, so bare her bow
  Diana's alone, so hit, and hunted so.

There's none so dull, that for your stile would ask,
    That saw you put on Pallas' plumed casque:
Or, keeping your due state, that would not cry,
    There Juno sat, and yet no peacock by.
So you are Nature's index, and restore,
    In yourself, all treasure lost of the age before.   20

CVI   *To Sir Edward Herbert*

If men get name, for some one virtue: then,
    What man art thou, that art so many men,
All-virtuous Herbert! On whose every part
    Truth might spend all her voice, fame all her art.
Whether thy learning they would take, or wit,
    Or valour, or thy judgement seasoning it,
Thy standing upright to thyself, thy ends
    Like straight, thy piety to God, and friends:
Their latter praise would still the greatest be,
    And yet, they, altogether, less than thee.   10

CVII   *To Captain Hungry*

Do what you come for, captain, with your news;
    That's, sit, and eat: do not my ears abuse.
I oft look on false coin, to know it from true:
    Not that I love it, more, than I will you.
Tell the gross Dutch those grosser tales of yours,
    How great you were with their two emperors;
And yet are with their princes: fill them full
    Of your Moravian horse, Venetian bull.
Tell them, what parts you've ta'en, whence run away,
    What states you've gull'd, and which yet keeps you in pay. 10
Give them your services, and embassies
    In Ireland, Holland, Sweden, pompous lies,

69

In Hungary, and Poland, Turkey too;
    What at Ligorne, Rome, Florence you did do:
And, in some year, all these together heap'd,
    For which there must more sea, and land be leap'd,
If but to be believ'd you have the hap,
    Than can a flea at twice skip in the map.
Give your young statesmen, (that first make you drunk,
    And then lie with you, closer, than a punk,   20
For news) your Villeroys, and Silleries,
    Janins, your nuncios, and your Tuilleries,
Your Arch-Dukes' agents, and your Beringhams,
    That are your words of credit. Keep your names
Of Hanou, Shieter-Huissen, Popenheim,
    Hans-spiegle, Rotteinberg, Boutersheim,
For your next meal: this you are sure of. Why
    Will you part with them, here, unthriftily?
Nay, now you puff, tusk, and draw up your chin,
    Twirl the poor chain you run a-feasting in.   30
Come, be not angry, you are Hungry; eat;
    Do what you come for, captain, there's your meat.

CVIII   *To True Soldiers*

Strength of my country, whilst I bring to view
    Such as are miscall'd captains, and wrong you;
And your high names: I do desire, that thence
    Be nor put on you, nor you take offence.
I swear by your true friend, my muse, I love
    Your great profession; which I once, did prove:
And did not shame it with my actions, then,
    No more, than I dare do now, with my pen.
He that not trusts me, having vow'd thus much,
    But's angry for the captain, still: is such.   10

CIX   *To Sir Henry Nevil*

Who now calls on thee, Nevil, is a muse,
   That serves nor fame, nor titles; but doth choose
Where virtue make them both, and that's in thee:
   Where all is fair, beside thy pedigree.
Thou art not one, seek'st miseries with hope,
   Wrestlest with dignities, or feign'st a scope
Of service to the public, when the end
   Is private gain, which hath long guilt to friend.
Thou rather striv'st the matter to possess,
   And elements of honour, than the dress;   10
To make thy lent life, good against the Fates:
   And first to know thine own state, then the State's.
To be the same in root, thou art in height;
   And that thy soul should give thy flesh her weight.
Go on, and doubt not, what posterity,
   Now I have sung thee thus, shall judge of thee.
Thy deeds, unto thy name, will prove new wombs,
   Whilst others toil for titles to their tombs.

CX   *To Clement Edmonds, on his CAESAR'S COMMENTARIES*
      observed, and translated

Not Caesar's deeds, not all his honours won,
   In these west parts, nor when that war was done,
The name of Pompey for an enemy,
   Cato's to boot, Rome, and her liberty,
All yielding to his fortune, nor, the while,
   To have engrav'd these acts, with his own stile,
And that so strong and deep, as't might be thought,
   He wrote, with the same spirit that he fought,
Nor that his works lived in the hands of foes,
   Un-argued then, and yet hath fame from those;   10
Not all these, Edmonds, or what else put to,
   Can so speak Caesar, as thy labours do.

For, where his person liv'd scarce one just age,
    And that, 'midst envy, and parts; then fell by rage:
His deeds too dying, but in books (whose good
    How few have read! How fewer understood?)
Thy learned hand, and true Promethean art
    (As by a new creation) part by part,
In every council, stratagem, design,
    Action, or engine, worth a note of thine,   20
To all future time, not only doth restore
    His life, but makes, that he can die no more.

CXI   *To the Same, on the Same*

Who Edmonds, reads thy book, and doth not see
    What the antique soldiers were, the modern be?
Wherein thou show'st, how much the latter are
    Beholding, to this master of the war;
And that, in action, there is nothing new,
    More, than to vary what our elders knew:
Which all, but ignorant captains will confess:
    Nor to give Caesar this, makes ours the less.
Yet thou, perhaps, shalt meet some tongues will grutch,
    That to the world thou should'st reveal so much,   10
And thence, deprave thee, and thy work. To those
    Caesar stands up, as from his urn late rose,
By thy great help: and doth proclaim by me,
    They murder him again, that envy thee.

CXII   *To a Weak Gamester in Poetry*

With thy small stock, why art thou vent'ring still,
    At this so subtle sport: and play'st so ill?
Think'st thou it is mere fortune, that can win?
    Or thy rank setting? That thou dar'st put in

Thy all, at all: and whatsoe'er I do,
    Art still at that, and think'st to blow me up too?
I cannot for the stage a drama lay,
    Tragic, or comic; but thou writ'st the play.
I leave thee there, and giving way, intend
    An epic poem; thou hast the same end.   **10**
I modestly quit that, and think to write,
    Next morning, an ode: thou mak'st a song ere night.
I pass to elegies; thou meet'st me there:
    To satires; and thou dost pursue me. Where,
Where shall I 'scape thee? In an epigram?
    O, (thou cry'st out) that is thy proper game.
Troth, if it be, I pity thy ill luck;
    That both for wit, and sense, so oft dost pluck,
And never art encounter'd, I confess:
    Nor scarce dost colour for it, which is less.   **20**
Prithee, yet save thy rest; give o'er in time:
    There's no vexation, that can make thee prime.

CXIII   *To Sir Thomas Overbury*

So Phoebus makes me worthy of his bays,
    As but to speak thee, Overbury, is praise:
So, where thou liv'st, thou mak'st life understood!
    Where, what makes others great, does keep thee good!
I think, the Fate of court thy coming crav'd,
    That the wit there, and manners might be sav'd:
For since, what ignorance, what pride is fled!
    And letters, and humanity in the stead!
Repent thee not of thy fair precedent,
    Could make such men, and such a place repent: **10**
Nor may any fear, to lose of their degree,
    Who in such ambition can but follow thee.

CXIV   *To Mrs Philip Sidney*

I must believe some miracles still be
   When Sidney's name I hear, or face I see:
For Cupid, who (at first) took vain delight,
   In mere out-forms, until he lost his sight,
Hath chang'd his soul, and made his object you:
   Where finding so much beauty met with virtue,
He hath not only gained himself his eyes,
   But, in your love, made all his servants wise.

CXV   *On the Town's Honest Man*

You wonder, who this is! And, why I name
   Him not, aloud, that boasts so good a fame:
Naming so many, too! But, this is one,
   Suffers no name, but a description:
Being no vicious person, but the vice
   About the town; and known too, at that price.
A subtle thing, that doth affections win
   By speaking well of the company it's in.
Talks loud, and bawdy, has a gather'd deal
   Of news, and noise, to sow out a long meal.   10
Can come from Tripoli, leap stools, and wink,
   Do all, that 'longs to the anarchy of drink,
Except the duel. Can sing songs, and catches;
   Give everyone his dose of mirth: and watches
Whose name's unwelcome to the present ear,
   And him it lays on; if he be not there.
Tells of him, all the tales, itself then makes;
   But, if it shall be question'd, undertakes,
It will deny all; and forswear it too:
   Not that it fears, but will not have to do   20
With such a one. And therein keeps its word.
   'Twill see its sister naked, ere a sword.

At every meal, where it doth dine, or sup,
    The cloth's no sooner gone, but it gets up
And, shifting of its faces, doth play more
    Parts, than the Italian could do, with his dore.
Acts old Iniquity, and in the fit
    Of miming, gets the opinion of a wit.
Executes men in picture. By defect,
    From friendship, is its own fame's architect.   30
An engineer, in slanders, of all fashions,
    That seeming praises, are, yet accusations.
Describ'd, it's thus: defin'd would you it have?
    Then, the town's honest man's her errant'st knave.

CXVI   *To Sir William Jephson*

Jephson, thou man of men, to whose lov'd name
    All gentry, yet, owe part of their best flame!
So did thy virtue inform, thy wit sustain
    That age, when thou stood'st up the master-brain:
Thou wert the first, mad'st merit know her strength,
    And those that lack'd it, to suspect at length,
'Twas not entail'd on title. That some word
    Might be found out as good, and not 'my lord'.
That Nature no such difference had impress'd
    In men, but every bravest was the best: 10
That blood not minds, but minds did blood adorn:
    And to live great, was better, than great born.
These were thy knowing arts: which who doth now
    Virtuously practise must at least allow
Them in, if not, from thee; or must commit
    A desperate solecism in truth and wit.

75

CXVII *On Groin*

Groin, come of age, his state sold out of hand
   For his whore: Groin does still occupy his land.

CXVIII *On Gut*

Gut eats all day, and lechers all the night,
   So all his meat he tasteth over, twice:
And, striving so to double his delight,
   He makes himself a thoroughfare of vice.
Thus, in his belly, can he change a sin,
   Lust it comes out, that gluttony went in.

CXIX *To Sir Ra(l)ph Shelton*

Not he that flies the court for want of clothes,
   At hunting rails, having no gift in oaths,
Cries out 'gainst cocking, since he cannot bet,
   Shuns prease, for two main causes, pox, and debt,
With me can merit more, than that good man,
   Whose dice not doing well, to a pulpit ran.
No, Shelton, give me thee, canst want all these,
   But dost it out of judgement, not disease;
Dar'st breath in any air; and with safe skill,
   Till thou canst find the best, choose the least ill.   10
That to the vulgar canst thyself apply,
   Treading a better path, not contrary;
And, in their errors' maze, thine own way know:
   Which is to live to conscience, not to show.
He, that, but living half his age, dies such;
   Makes the whole longer, than 'twas given him, much.

76

CXX   *Epitaph on S.P., a Child of Q. El(izabeth's) Chapel*

Weep with me all you that read
    This little story:
And know, for whom a tear you shed,
    Death's self is sorry.
'Twas a child, that so did thrive
    In grace, and feature,
As Heaven and Nature seem'd to strive
    Which own'd the creature.
Years he number'd scarce thirteen
    When Fates turn'd cruel,   10
Yet three fill'd zodiacs had he been
    The stage's jewel;
And did act (what now we moan)
    Old men so duly,
As, sooth, the Parcae thought him one,
    He play'd so truly.
So, by error, to his fate
    They all consented;
But viewing him since (alas, too late)
    They have repented.   20
And have sought (to give new birth)
    In baths to steep him;
But, being so much too good for earth,
    Heaven vows to keep him.

CXXI   *To Benjamin Rudyerd*

Rudyerd, as lesser dames, to great ones use,
    My lighter comes, to kiss thy learned muse;
Whose better studies while she emulates,
    She learns to know long difference of their states.
Yet is the office not to be despis'd,
    If only love should make the action priz'd:

77

Nor he, for friendship, to be thought unfit,
   That strives, his manners should procede his wit.

CXXII   *To the Same*

If I would wish, for truth, and not for show,
   The aged Saturn's age, and rites to know;
If I would strive to bring back times, and try
   The world's pure gold, and wise simplicity;
If I would virtue set, as she was young,
   And hear her speak with one, and her first tongue;
If holiest friendship, naked to the touch,
   I would restore, and keep it ever such,
I need no other arts, but study thee:
   Who prov'st, all these were, and again may be.   10

CXXIII   *To the Same*

Writing thyself, or judging others' writ,
   I know not which thou hast most, candour, or wit:
But both thou hast so, as who affects the state
   Of the best writer, and judge, should emulate.

CXXIV   *Epitaph on Elizabeth, L.H.*

Would'st thou hear, what man can say
   In a little? Reader, stay.
Underneath this stone doth lie
   As much beauty, as could die:
Which in life did harbour give
   To more virtue, than doth live.
If, at all, she had a fault,
   Leave it buried in this vault.

One name was Elizabeth,
   The other let it sleep with death:
Fitter, where it died, to tell,
   Than that it liv'd at all. Farewell.

CXXV   *To Sir William Uvedale*

Uvedale, thou piece of the first times, a man
   Made for what Nature could, or virtue can;
Both whose dimensions, lost, the world might find
   Restored in thy body, and thy mind!
Who sees a soul, in such a body set,
   Might love the treasure for the cabinet.
But I, no child, no fool, respect the kind,
   The flowing graces there enshrin'd;
Which (would the world not miscall't flattery)
   I could adore, almost t'idolatry.   10

CXXVI   *To His Lady, then Mrs Cary*

Retir'd, with purpose your fair worth to praise,
   'Mongst Hampton shades, and Phoebus' grove of bays,
I pluck'd a branch; the jealous god did frown,
   And bad me lay the usurped laurel down:
Said I wrong'd him, and (which was more) his love.
   I answer'd, 'Daphne now no pain can prove.'
Phoebus replied. 'Bold head, it is not she:
   Cary my love is, Daphne but my tree.'

CXXVII   *To Esmé, Lord Aubigny*

Is there hope, that man would thankful be,
   If I should fail, in gratitude, to thee

To whom I am so bound, lov'd Aubigny?
  No, I do, therefore, call posterity
Into the debt; and reckon on her head,
  How full of want, how swallow'd up, how dead
I, and this muse had been, if thou hadst not
  Lent timely succours, and new life begot:
So, all reward, or name, that grows to me
  By her attempt, shall still be owing thee.   10
And, than this same, I know no abler way
  To thank thy benefits: which is, to pay.

CXXVIII   *To William Roe*

Roe (and my joy to name) thou art now, to go
  Countries, and climes, manners, and men to know,
To extract, and choose the best of all these known,
  And those to turn to blood, and make thine own:
May winds as soft as breath of kissing friends,
  Attend thee hence; and there, may all thy ends,
As the beginnings here, prove purely sweet,
  And perfect in a circle always meet.
So, when we, blest with thy return, shall see
  Thyself, with thy first thoughts, brought home by thee,   10
We each to other may this voice inspire;
  This is that good Aeneas, pass'd through fire,
Through seas, storms, tempests: and embark'd for hell,
  Came back untouch'd. This man hath travell'd well.

CXXIX   *To Mime*

That, not a pair of friends each other see,
  But the first question is, when one saw thee?
That there's no journey set, or thought upon,
  To Brainford, Hackney, Bow, but thou mak'st one;

That scarce the town designeth any feast
    To which th'art not a week, bespoke a guest;
That still th'art made the supper's flag, the drum,
    The very call, to make all others come:
Think'st thou, Mime, this is great? Or, that they strive
    Whose noise shall keep thy miming most alive,   10
Whilst thou dost raise some player, from the grave,
    Outdance the babion, or out-boast the brave;
Or (mounted on a stool) thy face doth hit
    On some new gesture, that's imputed wit?
O, run not proud of this. Yet, take thy due.
    Thou dost out-zany Cokely, Pod; nay, Gue:
And thine own Coriat too. But (would'st thou see)
    Men love thee not for this: they laugh at thee.

CXXX   *To Alphonso Ferrabosco, on his Book*

To urge, my lov'd Alphonso, that bold fame,
    Of building towns, and making wild beasts tame,
Which music had; or speak her known effects,
    That she removeth cares, sadness ejects,
Declineth anger, persuades clemency,
    Doth sweeten mirth, and heighten piety,
And as t'a body, often, ill inclin'd,
    No less a sovereign cure, than to the mind;
To allege, that greatest men were not asham'd,
    Of old, even by her practice to be fam'd;   10
To say, indeed, she were the soul of heaven,
    That the eight spheres, no less, than planets seven,
Mov'd by her order, and the ninth more high,
    Including all, were thence called harmony:
I, yet, had utter'd nothing on thy part,
    When these were but the praises of the art.
But when I have said, the proofs of all these be
    Shed in thy songs; 'tis true: but short of thee.

CXXXI *To the Same*

When we do give, Alphonso, to the light,
   A work of ours, we part with our own right;
For, then, all mouths will judge, and their own way:
   The learn'd have no more privilege, than the lay.
And though we could all men, all censures hear,
   We ought not give them taste, we had an ear.
For, if the humorous world will talk at large,
   They should be fools, for me, at their own charge.
Say, this, or that man they to thee prefer;
   Even those for whom they do this, know they err: 10
And would (being ask'd the truth) ashamed say,
   They were not to be nam'd on the same day.
Then stand unto thyself, not seek without
   For fame, with breath soon kindled, soon blown out.

CXXXII *To Mr Joshua Sylvester*

If to admire were to commend, my praise
   Might then both thee, thy work and merit raise:
But, as it is (the child of ignorance,
   And utter stranger to all airs of France)
How can I speak of thy great pains, but err?
   Since they can only judge, that can confer.
Behold! The reverend shade of Bartas stands
   Before my thought, and (in thy right) commands
That to the world I publish, for him, this;
   Bartas doth wish thy English now were his.   10
So well in that are his inventions wrought,
   As his will now be the translation thought,
Thine the original; and France shall boast,
   No more, those maiden glories she hath lost.

CXXXIII   *On The Famous Voyage*

No more let Greece her bolder fables tell
  Of Hercules, or Theseus going to hell,
Orpheus, Ulysses: or the Latin muse,
  With tales of Troy's just knight, our faiths abuse:
We have a Shelton, and a Heyden got,
  Had power to act, what they to feign had not.
All, that they boast of Styx, of Acheron,
  Cocytus, Phlegeton, our have prov'd in one;
The filth, stench, noise: save only what was there
  Subtly distinguish'd, was confused here.   10
Their wherry had no sail, too; ours had none:
  And in it, two more horrid knaves, than Charon.
Arses were heard to croak, instead of frogs;
  And for one Cerberus, the whole coast was dogs.
Furies there wanted not: each scold was ten.
  And, for the cries of ghosts, women, and men,
Laden with plague-sores, and their sins, were heard,
  Lash'd by their consciences, to die, afeard.
Then let the former age, with this content her,
  She brought the poets forth, but ours the adventer.   20

The Voyage Itself

I sing the brave adventure of two wights
And pity 'tis, I cannot call'em knights:
One was; and he, for brawn, and brain, right able
To have been styled of King Arthur's table.
The other was a squire, of fair degree;
But, in the action, greater man than he:
Who gave, to take at his return from Hell,
His three for one. Now, lordings, listen well.
  It was the day, what time the powerful moon
Makes the poor Bankside creature wet its shoon,   30

83

In its own hall; when these (in worthy scorn
Of those, that put out moneys, on return
From Venice, Paris, or some inland passage
Of six times to, and fro, without embassage,
Or him that backward went to Berwick, or which
Did dance the famous Morris, unto Norwich)
At Bread Street's Mermaid, having din'd, and merry,
Propos'd to go to Holborn in a wherry:
A harder task, than either his to Bristo',
Or his to Antwerp. Therefore, once more, list ho.   40
   A dock there is, that called is Avernus,
Of some Bridewell, and may, in time, concern us
All, that are readers: but, methinks 'tis odd,
That all this while I have forgot some god,
Or goddess to invoke, to stuff my verse;
And with both bombard style, and phrase, rehearse
The many perils of this port, and how
Sans help of Sybil, or a golden bough,
Or magic sacrifice, they pass'd along!
Alcides, be thou succouring to my song.   50
Thou hast seen hell (some say) and know'st all nooks there,
Canst tell me best, how every Fury looks there,
And art a god, if Fame thee not abuses,
Always at hand, to aid the merry muses.
Great club-fist, though my back, and bones be sore,
Still, with thy former labours; yet, once more,
Act a brave work, call it thy last adventry:
But hold my torch, while I describe the entry
To this dire passage. Say, thou stop thy nose:
'Tis but light pains: indeed this dock's no rose.   60
   In the first jaws appear'd that ugly monster,
Ycleped Mud, which, when their oars did once stir,
Belch'd forth an air, as hot, as at the muster
Of all your night-tubs, when the carts do cluster,
Who shall discharge first his merd-urinous load:
Thorough her womb they make their famous road,

Between two walls; where, on one side, to scar men,
Were seen your ugly centaurs, ye call car-men,
Gorgonian scolds, and harpies: on the other
Hung stench, diseases, and old filth, their mother,   70
With famine, wants, and sorrows many a dozen,
The least of which was to the plague a cousin.
But they unfrighted pass, though many a privy
Spake to'em louder, than the ox in Livy;
And many a sink pour'd out her rage anenst'em;
But still their valour, and their virtue fenc'd'em,
And, on they went, like Castor brave and Pollux:
Ploughing the main. When, see (the worst of all lucks)
They met the second prodigy, would fear a
Man, that had never heard of a Chimera.   80
One said, it was bold Briareus, or the beadle,
(Who hath the hundred hands when he doth meddle)
The other thought it Hydra, or the rock
Made of the trull, that cut her father's lock:
But, coming near, they found it but a lighter,
So huge, it seem'd, they could by no means quit her.
'Back,' cried their brace of Charons: they cried, 'No,
No going back; on still you rogues, and row.'
'How hight the place?' A voice was heard, 'Cocytus.'
'Row close then slaves.' 'Alas, they will beshite us.'   90
'No matter, stinkards, row.' 'What croaking sound
Is this we hear. Of frogs?' 'No, guts wind-bound,
Over your heads: well, row.' At this a loud
Crack did report itself, as if a cloud
Had burst with storm, and down fell, *ab excelsis*,
Poor Mercury, crying out on Paracelsus,
And all his followers, that had so abus'd him:
And in so shitten sort, so long had us'd him:
For (where he was the god of eloquence,
And subtlety of metals) they dispense   100
His spirits, now, in pills, and eek in potions,
Suppositories, cataplasms, and lotions.

85

But many moons there shall not wane (quoth he)
(In the meantime, let'em imprison me)
But I will speak (and know I shall be heard)
Touching this cause, where they will be afear'd
To answer me. And sure, it was the intent
Of the great fart, late let in parliament,
Had it been seconded, and not in fume
Vanish'd away: as you must all presume   110
Their Mercury did now. By this, the stem
Of the hulk touch'd, and, as by Polypheme
The sly Ulysses stole in a sheepskin,
The well-greas'd wherry now had got between,
And bad her farewell sough, unto the lurden:
Never did bottom more betray her burden;
The meat-boat of Bear's college, Paris garden,
Stunk not so ill; nor, when she kiss'd, Kate Arden.
Yet, one day in the year, for sweet 'tis voic'd,
And that is when it is the Lord Mayor's foist.   120
   By this time had they reach'd the Stygian pool,
By which the masters swear, when, on the stool
Of worship, they their nodding chins do hit
Against their breasts. Here, several ghosts did flit
About the shore, of farts, but late departed,
White, black, blue, green, and in more forms out-started,
Than all those *atomi* ridiculous,
Whereof old Democrite, and Hill Nicholas,
One said, the other swore, the world consists.
These be the cause of those thick frequent mists   130
Arising in that place, through which, who goes,
Must try the unused valour of a nose:
And that ours did. For, yet, no nare was tainted,
Nor thumb, nor finger to the stop acquainted,
But open, and unarm'd encounter'd all:
Whether it languishing stuck upon the wall,
Or were precipitated down the jakes,
And, after, swom abroad in ample flakes,

86

Or, that it lay, heap'd like an usurer's mass,
All was to them the same, they were to pass,   140
And so they did, from Styx, to Acheron:
The ever-boiling flood. Whose banks upon
Your Fleet Lane Furies; and hot cooks do dwell,
That, with still-scalding steams, make the place hell.
The sinks ran grease, and hair of measled hogs,
The heads, houghs, entrails, and the hides of dogs:
For, to say truth, what scullion is so nasty,
To put the skins, and offal in a pasty?
Cats there lay divers had been flay'd, and roasted,
And, after mouldy grown, again were toasted,   150
Then, selling not, a dish was ta'en to mince'em,
But still, it seem'd, the rankness did convince'em.
For, here they were thrown in with the melted pewter,
Yet drown'd they not. They had five lives in future.
   But 'mongst these Tiberts, who do you think there was?
Old Banks the juggler, our Pythagoras,
Grave tutor to the learned horse. Both which,
Being, beyond sea, burned for one witch:
Their spirits transmigrated to a cat:
And, now, above the pool, a face right fat   160
With great grey eyes, are lifted up, and mew'd;
Thrice did it spit: thrice div'd. At last, it view'd
Our brave heroes with a milder glare,
And, in a piteous tune, began. 'How dare
Your dainty nostrils (in so hot a season,
When every clerk eats artichoke, and peason,
Laxative lettuce, and such windy meat)
'Tempt such a passage? When each privy's seat
Is fill'd with buttock? And the walls to sweat
Urine, and plasters? When the noise doth beat   170
Upon your ears, of discords so unsweet?
And outcries of the damned in the Fleet?
Cannot the plague-bill keep you back? Nor bells
Of loud sepulchres with their hourly knells,

But you will visit grisly Pluto's hall?
Behold where Cerberus, rear'd on the wall
Of Holborn (three sergeants' heads) looks o'er,
And stays but till you come unto the door!
Tempt not his fury, Pluto is away:
And Madam Caesar, great Proserpina,   180
Is now from home. You lose your labours quite,
Were you Jove's sons, or had Alcides' might.'
They cried out Puss. He told them he was Banks,
That had, so often, show'd'em merry pranks.
They laugh'd, at his laugh-worthy fate. And pass'd
The triple head without a sop. At last,
Calling for Radamanthus, that dwelt by,
A soap-boiler; and Aeacus him nigh,
Who kept an ale-house; with my little Minos,
An ancient purblind fletcher, with a high nose;   190
They took'em all to witness of their action:
And so went bravely back, without protraction.
   In memory of which most liquid deed,
The city since hath rais'd a pyramid.
And I could wish for their eterniz'd sakes,
My muse had plough'd with his, that sung A-JAX.

The Forest

I   *Why I Write Not of Love*

Some act of Love's bound to rehearse,
I thought to bind him, in my verse:
Which when he felt, Away (quoth he)
Can poets hope to fetter me?
It is enough, they once did get
Mars, and my mother, in their net:
I wear not these my wings in vain.
With which he fled me: and again,
Into my rhymes could ne'er be got
By any art. Then wonder not,   10
That since, my numbers are so cold,
When Love is fled, and I grow old.

II   *To Penshurst*

Thou art not, Penshurst, built to envious show,
    Of touch, or marble; nor canst boast a row
Of polish'd pillars, or a roof of gold:
    Thou hast no lanthern, whereof tales are told;
Or stair, or courts; but stand'st an ancient pile,
    And these grudg'd at, art reverenc'd the while.
Thou joy'st in better marks, of soil, of air,
    Of wood, of water: therein thou art fair.
Thou hast thy walks for health, as well as sport:
    Thy Mount, to which the dryads do resort,   10
Where Pan, and Bacchus their high feasts have made,
    Beneath the broad beech, and the chestnut shade;
That taller tree, which of a nut was set,
    At his great birth, where all the muses met.
There in the writhed bark, are cut the names
    Of many a sylvan, taken with his flames.
And thence, the ruddy satyrs oft provoke
    The lighter fauns, to reach thy Lady's Oak.

91

Thy copse, too, nam'd of Gamage, thou hast there,
    That never fails to serve thee season'd deer,   20
When thou would'st feast, or exercise thy friends.
    The lower land, that to the river bends,
Thy sheep, thy bullocks, kine, and calves do feed:
    The middle grounds thy mares, and horses breed.
Each bank doth yield thee conies; and the tops
    Fertile of wood, Ashore, and Sidney's copse,
To crown thy open table, doth provide
    The purpled pheasant, with the speckled side:
The painted partridge lies in every field,
    And, for thy mess, is willing to be kill'd.   30
And if the high-swoll'n Medway fail thy dish,
    Thou hast thy ponds, that pay thee tribute fish,
Fat, aged carps, that run into thy net.
    And pikes, now weary their own kind to eat,
As loth, the second draught, or cast to stay,
    Officiously, at first, themselves betray.
Bright eels, that emulate them, and leap on land,
    Before the fisher, or into his hand.
Then hath thy orchard fruit, thy garden flowers,
    Fresh as the air, and new as are the hours.   40
The early cherry, with the later plum,
    Fig, grape, and quince, each in his time doth come:
The blushing apricot, and woolly peach
    Hang on thy walls, that every child may reach.
And though thy walls be of the country stone,
    They're rear'd with no man's ruin, no man's groan,
There's none, that dwell about them, wish them down;
    But all come in, the farmer, and the clown:
And no one empty-handed, to salute
    Thy lord, and lady, though they have no suit.   50
Some bring a capon, some a rural cake,
    Some nuts, some apples; some that think they make
The better cheeses, bring'em; or else send
    By their ripe daughters, whom they would commend

This way to husbands; and whose baskets bear
    An emblem of themselves, in plum, or pear.
But what can this (more than express their love)
    Add to thy free provisions, far above
The need of such? Whose liberal board doth flow,
    With all, that hospitality doth know!   60
Where comes no guest, but is allow'd to eat,
    Without his fear, and of the lord's own meat:
Where the same beer, and bread, and self-same wine,
    That is his lordship's, shall be also mine.
And I not fain to sit (as some, this day,
    At great men's tables) and yet dine away.
Here no man tells my cups; nor, standing by,
    A waiter, doth my gluttony envy:
But gives me what I call, and lets me eat,
    He knows, below, he shall find plenty of meat,   70
Thy tables hoard not up for the next day,
    Nor, when I take my lodging, need I pray
For fire, or lights, or livery: all is there;
    As if thou, then, wert mine, or I reign'd here:
There's nothing I can wish, for which I stay.
    That found King James, when hunting late, this way,
With his brave son, the prince, they saw thy fires
    Shine bright on every hearth as the desires
Of thy *Penates* had been set on flame,
    To entertain them; or the country came,   80
With all their zeal, to warm their welcome here.
    What (great, I will not say, but) sudden cheer
Did'st thou, then, make'em! and what praise was heap'd
    On thy good lady, then! who therein reap'd
The just reward of her high huswifery;
    To have her linen, plate, and all things nigh,
When she was far: and not a room, but dress'd,
    As if it had expected such a guest!
These, Penshurst, are thy praise, and yet not all.
    Thy lady's noble, fruitful, chaste withal.   90

93

His children thy great lord may call his own:
    A fortune, in this age, but rarely known.
They are, and have been taught religion: thence
    Their gentler spirits have suck'd innocence.
Each morn, and even, they are taught to pray,
    With the whole household, and may, every day,
Read, in their virtuous parents' noble parts,
    The mysteries of manners, arms, and arts.
Now, Penshurst, they that will proportion thee
    With other edifices, when they see   100
Those proud, ambitious heaps, and nothing else,
    May say, their lords have built, but thy lord dwells.

III   *To Sir Robert Wroth*

How blest art thou, canst love the country, Wroth,
    Whether by choice, or fate, or both;
And, though so near the city, and the court,
    Art ta'en with neither's vice, nor sport:
That at great times, art no ambitious guest
    Of sheriff's dinner, or mayor's feast.
Nor com'st to view the better cloth of state;
    The richer hangings, or crown-plate;
Nor throng'st (when masquing is) to have a sight
    Of the short bravery of the night;   10
To view the jewels, stuffs, the pains, the wit
    There wasted, some not paid for yet!
But canst, at home, in thy securer rest,
    Live, with un-bought provision blest;
Free from proud porches, or their gilded roofs,
    'Mongst lowing herds, and solid hoofs:
Alongst the curled woods, and painted meads,
    Through which a serpent river leads
To some cool, courteous shade, which he calls his,
    And makes sleep softer than it is!   20

Or, if thou list the night in watch to break,
   A-bed canst hear the loud stag speak,
In spring, oft roused for thy master's sport,
   Who, for it, makes thy house his court;
Or with thy friends; the heart of all the year,
   Divid'st, upon the lesser deer;
In autumn, at the partridge makes a flight,
   And giv'st thy gladder guests the sight;
And, in the winter, hunt'st the flying hare,
   More for thy exercise, than fare;   30
While all, that follow, their glad ears apply
   To the full greatness of the cry:
Or hawking at the river, or the bush,
   Or shooting at the greedy thrush,
Thou dost with some delight the day out-wear
   Although the coldest of the year!
The whilst, the several seasons thou hast seen
   Of flow'ry fields, of copses green,
The mowed meadows, with the fleeced sheep,
   And feasts, that either shearers keep;   40
The ripened ears, yet humble in their height,
   And furrows laden with their weight;
The apple-harvest, that doth longer last;
   The hogs return'd home fat from mast;
The trees cut out in log; and those boughs made
   A fire now, that lent a shade!
Thus Pan, and Sylvan, having had their rites,
   Comus puts in, for new delights;
And fills thy open hall with mirth, and cheer,
   As if in Saturn's reign it were;   50
Apollo's harp, and Hermes' lyre resound,
   Nor are the muses strangers found:
The rout of rural folk come thronging in,
   (Their rudeness then is thought no sin)
Thy noblest spouse affords them welcome grace;
   And the great heroes, of her race,

Sit mix'd with loss of state, or reverence.
 Freedom doth with degree dispense.
The jolly wassail walks the often round,
 And in their cups, their cares are drown'd: 60
They think not, then, which side the cause shall leese,
 Nor how to get the lawyer fees.
Such, and no other was that age, of old,
 Which boasts t'have had the head of gold.
And such since thou canst make thine own content,
 Strive, Wroth, to live long innocent.
Let others watch in guilty arms, and stand
 The fury of a rash command,
Go enter breaches, meet the cannon's rage,
 That they may sleep with scars in age.   70
And show their feathers shot, and colours torn,
 And brag, that they were therefore born.
Let this man sweat, and wrangle at the bar,
 For every price, in every jar,
And change possessions, oft'ner with his breath,
 Than either money, war, or death:
Let him, than hardest sires, more disinherit,
 And eachwhere boast it as his merit,
To blow up orphans, widows, and their states;
 And think his power doth equal Fate's.   80
Let that go heap a mass of wretched wealth,
 Purchas'd by rapine, worse than stealth,
And brooding o'er it sit, with broadest eyes,
 Not doing good, scarce when he dies.
Let thousands more go flatter vice, and win,
 By being organs to great sin,
Get place, and honour, and be glad to keep
 The secrets, that shall break their sleep:
And, so they ride in purple, eat in plate,
 Though poison, think it a great fate.   90
But thou, my Wroth, if I can truth apply,
 Shalt neither that, nor this envy:

96

Thy peace is made; and, when man's state is well,
   'Tis better, if he there can dwell.
God wisheth, none should wrack on a strange shelf:
   To him, man's dearer, than t'himself.
And, howsoever we may think things sweet,
   He always gives what he knows meet;
Which who can use is happy: such be thou.
   Thy morning's, and thy evening's vow   100
Be thanks to him, and earnest prayer, to find
   A body sound, with sounder mind;
To do thy country service, thyself right;
   That neither want do thee affright,
Nor death; but when thy latest sand is spent,
   Thou mayst think life, a thing but lent.

IV   *To the World: a farewell for a gentlewoman, virtuous and noble*

False world, good-night: since thou hast brought
   That hour upon my morn of age,
Henceforth I quit thee from my thought,
   My part is ended on thy stage.
Do not once hope, that thou canst tempt
   A spirit so resolv'd to tread
Upon thy throat, and live exempt
   From all the nets that thou canst spread.
I know thy forms are studied arts,
   Thy subtle ways, be narrow straits;   10
Thy courtesy but sudden starts,
   And what thou call'st thy gifts are baits.
I know too, though thou strut, and paint,
   Yet art thou both shrunk up, and old,
That only fools make thee a saint,
   And all thy good is to be sold.
I know thou whole art but a shop
   Of toys, and trifles, traps, and snares,

To take the weak, or make them stop:
   Yet art thou falser than thy wares.   20
And, knowing this, should I yet stay,
   Like such as blow away their lives,
And never will redeem a day,
   Enamour'd of their golden gyves?
Or, having 'scap'd, shall I return,
   And thrust my neck into the noose,
From whence, so lately, I did burn,
   With all my powers, myself to loose?
What bird, or beast, is known so dull,
   That fled his cage, or broke his chain,   30
And tasting air, and freedom, wull
   Render his head in there again?
If these, who have but sense, can shun
   The engines, that have them annoy'd;
Little, for me, had reason done,
   If I could not thy gins avoid.
Yes, threaten, do. Alas I fear
   As little, as I hope from thee:
I know thou canst nor show, nor bear
   More hatred, than thou hast to me.   40
My tender, first, and simple years
   Thou did'st abuse, and then betray;
Since stirred'st up jealousies and fears,
   When all the causes were away.
Then, in a soil hath planted me,
   Where breathe the basest of thy fools;
Where envious arts professed be,
   And pride, and ignorance the schools,
Where nothing is examin'd, weigh'd,
   But, as 'tis rumour'd, so believ'd: 50
Where every freedom is betray'd,
   And every goodness tax'd, or griev'd.
But, what we're born for, we must bear:
   Our frail condition it is such,

That, what to all may happen here,
   If't chance to me, I must not grutch.
Else, I my state should much mistake,
   To harbour a divided thought
From all my kind: that, for my sake,
   There should a miracle be wrought.   60
No, I do not know, that I was born
   To age, misfortune, sickness, grief:
But I will bear these, with that scorn,
   As shall not need thy false relief.
Nor for my peace will I go far,
   As wand'rers do, that still do roam,
But make my strengths, such as they are,
   Here in my bosom, and at home.

V   *Song: To Celia*

Come my Celia, let us prove,
While we may, the sports of love;
Time will not be ours, for ever:
He, at length, our good will sever.
Spend not then his gifts in vain.
Suns, that set, may rise again:
But if once we lose this light,
'Tis, with us, perpetual night.
Why should we defer our joys?
Fame, and rumour are but toys.   10
Cannot we delude the eyes
Of a few poor household spies?
Or his easier ears beguile,
So removed by our wile?
'Tis no sin, love's fruit to steal,
But the sweet theft to reveal:
To be taken, to be seen,
These have crimes accounted been.

99

VI *To the Same*

Kiss me, sweet: the wary lover,
Can your favours keep, and cover,
When the common courting jay
All your bounties will betray.
Kiss again: no creature comes.
Kiss, and score up wealthy sums
On my lips, thus hardly sund'red,
While you breathe. First give a hundred,
Then a thousand, then another
Hundred, then unto the tother   10
Add a thousand, and so more:
Till you equal with the store,
All the grass that Romney yields,
Or the sands in Chelsea fields,
Or the drops in silver Thames,
Or the stars, that gild his streams,
In the silent summer nights,
When youths ply their stol'n delights.
That the curious may not know
How to tell'em, as they flow,   20
And the envious, when they find
What their number is, be pin'd.

VII *Song: That Women Are But Men's Shadows*

Follow a shadow, it still flies you;
   Seem to fly it, it will pursue:
So court a mistress, she denies you;
   Let her alone, she will court you.
Say, are not women truly, then,
   Styl'd but the shadows of us men?
At morn, and even, shades are longest;
   At noon, they are or short or none:

So men at weakest, they are strongest,
    But grant us perfect, they're not known.   10
Say, are not women truly, then,
    Styl'd but the shadows of us men?

VIII   *To Sickness*

Why, Disease, dost thou molest
Ladies? and of them the best?
Do not men, enow of rites
To thy altars, by their nights
Spent in surfeits: and their days,
And nights too, in worser ways?
    Take heed, Sickness, what you do,
    I shall fear, you'll surfeit too.
Live not we, as, all thy stalls,
Spittles, pest-house, hospitals,   10
Scarce will take our present store?
    And this age will build no more:
'Pray thee, feed contented, then,
Sickness; only on us men.
    Or if needs thy lust will taste
    Womankind; devour the waste
    Livers, round about the town.
But, forgive me, with thy crown
They maintain the truest trade,
And have more diseases made.   20
    What should, yet, thy palate please?
    Daintiness, and softer ease,
    Sleeked limbs, and finest blood?
    If thy leanness love such food,
    There are those, that, for thy sake,
    Do enough; and who would take
    Any pains; yea, think it price,
    To become thy sacrifice.

That distil their husbands' land
In decoctions; and are mann'd   30
With ten emp'rics, in their chamber,
Lying for the spirit of amber.
That for the oil of Talc, dare spend
More than citizens dare lend
Them, and all their officers.
That, to make all pleasures theirs,
Will by coach, and water go,
Every stew in town to know;
Dare entail their loves on any,
Bald, or blind, or ne'er so many: 40
And, for thee, at common game,
Play away, health, wealth, and fame.
These, Disease, will thee deserve:
And will, long ere thou should'st starve
On their beds, most prostitute,
Move it, as their humblest suit,
In thy justice to molest
None but them, and leave the rest.

IX   *Song: To Celia*

Drink to me, only, with thine eyes,
    And I will pledge with mine;
Or leave a kiss but in the cup,
    And I'll not look for wine.
The thirst, that from the soul doth rise,
    Doth ask a drink divine:
But might I of Jove's *nectar* sup,
    I would not change for thine.
I sent thee, late, a rosie wreath,
    Not so much honouring thee,   10
As giving it a hope, that there
    It could not withered be,

102

But thou thereon did'st only breathe,
    And sent'st it back to me:
Since when it grows, and smells, I swear,
    Not of itself, but thee.

X

And must I sing? What subject shall I choose?
Or whose great name in poets' heaven use?
For the more countenance to my active muse?

Hercules? Alas his bones are yet sore,
With his old earthly labours. T'exact more,
Of his dull god-head, were sin. I'll implore

Phoebus. No? Tend thy cart still. Envious day
Shall not give out, that I have made thee stay,
And found'red thy hot team, to tune my lay.

Nor will I beg of thee, lord of the vine,   10
To raise my spirits with thy conjuring wine,
In the green circle of thy ivy twine.

Pallas, nor thee I call on, mankind maid,
That, at thy birth, mad'st the poor smith afraid,
Who, with his axe, thy father's midwife play'd.

Go, cramp dull Mars, light Venus, when he snorts,
Or, with thy tribute trine, invent new sports,
Thou, nor thy looseness with my making sorts.

Let the old boy, your son, ply his old task,
Turn the stale prologue to some painted masque,   20
His absence in my verse, is all I ask.

Hermes, the cheater, shall not mix with us,
Though he would steal his sisters' Pegasus,
And riffle him: or pawn his Petasus.

Nor all the ladies of the Thespian lake,
(Though they were crush'd into one form) could make
A beauty of that merit, that should take

My muse up by commission: no, I bring
My own true fire. Now my thought takes wing,
And now an epode to deep ears I sing.   30

XI *Epode*

Not to know vice at all, and keep true state,
    Is virtue, and not Fate:
Next, to that virtue, is to know vice well,
    And her black spite expell.
Which to effect (since no breast is so sure,
    Or safe, but she'll procure
Some way of entrance) we must plant a guard
    Of thoughts to watch, and ward
As th'eye and ear (the ports unto the mind)
    That no strange, or unkind   10
Object arrive there, but the heart (our spy)
    Give knowledge instantly,
To wakeful reason, our affections' king:
    Who (in th'examining)
Will quickly taste the treason, and commit
    Close, the close cause of it.
'Tis the securest policy we have,
    To make our sense our slave.
But this true course is not embrac'd by many:
    By many? Scarce by any.   20

For either our affections do rebel,
        Or else the sentinel
(That should ring 'larum to the heart) doth sleep,
        Or some great thought doth keep
Back the intelligence, and falsely swears,
        They're base, and idle fears
Whereof the loyal conscience so complains.
        Thus, by these subtle trains,
Do several passions invade the mind,
        And strike our reason blind.   30
Of which usurping rank, some have thought love
        The first; as prone to move
Most frequent tumults, horrors, and unrests,
        In our inflamed breasts:
But this doth from the cloud of error grow,
        Which thus we over-blow.
The thing, they here call love, is blind desire,
        Arm'd with bow, shafts, and fire;
Inconstant, like the sea, of whence 'tis born,
        Rough, swelling, like a storm: 40
With whom who sails, rides on the surge of fear,
        And boils, as if he were
In a continual tempest. Now, true love
        No such effects doth prove;
That is an essence, far more gentle, fine,
        Pure, perfect, nay divine;
It is a golden chain let down from heaven,
        Whose links are bright, and even,
That falls like sleep on lovers, and combines
        The soft, and sweetest minds   50
In equal knots: this bears no brands, nor darts,
        To murther different hearts,
But, in a calm, and god-like unity,
        Preserves community.
O, who is he, that (in this peace) enjoys
        Th'elixir of all joys?

105

A form more fresh, than are the Eden bowers
    And lasting, as her flowers:
Richer than time, and as time's virtue, rare.
    Sober, as saddest care: 60
A fixed thought, an eye un-taught to glance;
    Who (blest with such high chance)
Would, at suggestion of a steep desire,
    Cast himself from the spire
Of all his happiness? But soft: I hear
    Some vicious fool draw near,
That cries, we dream, and swears, there's no such thing,
    As this chaste love we sing.
Peace luxury, thou art like one of those
    Who, being at sea, suppose   70
Because they move, the continent doth so:
    No, vice, we let thee know
Though thy wild thoughts with sparrows' wings do fly,
    Turtles can chastely die;
And yet (in this t'express ourselves more clear)
    We do not number, here,
Such spirits as are only continent,
    Because lust's means are spent:
Or those, who doubt the common mouth of fame,
    And for their place, and name,   .   80
Cannot so safely sin. Their chastity
    Is mere necessity.
Nor mean we those, whom vows and conscience
    Have fill'd with abstinence:
Though we acknowledge, who can so abstain,
    Makes a most blessed gain.
He that for love of goodness hateth ill,
    Is more crown-worthy still,
Than he, which for sin's penalty forbears.
    His heart sins, though he fears.   90
But we propose a person like our dove,
    Grac'd with a phoenix love;

A beauty of that clear, and sparkling light,
    Would make a day of night,
And turn the blackest sorrows to bright joys:
    Whose od'rous breath destroys
All taste of bitterness, and makes the air
    As sweet, as she is fair.
A body so harmoniously compos'd,
    As if Nature disclos'd   100
All her best symmetry in that one feature!
    O, so divine a creature
Who could be false to? Chiefly, when he knows
    How only she bestows
The wealthy treasure of her love on him;
    Making his fortunes swim
In the full flood of her admir'd perfection?
    What savage, brute affection,
Would not be fearful to offend a dame
    Of this excelling frame?   110
Much more a noble, and right generous mind
    (To virtuous moods inclin'd)
That knows the weight of guilt: he will refrain
    From thoughts of such a strain.
And to his sense object this sentence ever,
    Man may securely sin, but safely never.

XII   *Epistle to Elizabeth, Countess of Rutland*

Madam,
Whil'st that, for which, all virtue now is sold,
    And almost every vice, almighty gold,
That which, to boot with hell, is thought worth heaven,
    And, for it, life, conscience, yes, souls are given,
Toils, by grave custom, up and down the court,
    To every squire, or groom, that will report

Well, or ill, only, all the following year,
    Just to the weight their this-day's-presents bear;
While it makes ushers serviceable men,
    And someone apteth to be trusted, then,   10
Though never after; whiles it gains the voice
    Of some grand peer, whose air doth make rejoice
The fool that gave it; who will want, and weep,
    When his proud patron's favours are asleep;
While thus it buys great grace, and hunts poor fame;
    Runs between man, and man; 'tween dame, and dame;
Solders crack'd friendship; makes love last a day;
    Or perhaps less: whilst gold bears all this sway,
I, that have none (to send you) send you verse.
    A present, which (if elder writs rehearse   20
The truth of times) was once of more esteem,
    Than this, our guilt, nor golden age can deem,
When gold was made no weapon to cut throats,
    Or put to flight Astraea, when her ingots
Were yet unfound, and better plac'd in earth,
    Than, here, to give pride fame, and peasants birth.
But let this dross carry what price it will
    With noble ignorants, and let them still,
Turn, upon scorned verse, their quarter-face:
    With you, I know, my off'ring will find grace.   30
For what a sin 'gainst your great father's spirit,
    Were it to think, that you should not inherit
His love unto the muses, when his skill
    Almost you have, or may have, when you will?
Wherein wise Nature you a dow'ry gave,
    Worth an estate, treble to that you have.
Beauty, I know, is good, and blood is more;
    Riches thought most; but, madam, think what store
The world hath seen, which all these had in trust,
    And now lie lost in their forgotten dust.   40
It is the muse, alone, can raise to heaven,
    And at her strong arms' end, hold up, and even,

The souls, she loves. Those other glorious notes,
    Inscrib'd in touch or marble, or the coats
Painted, or carv'd upon our great-men's tombs,
    Or in their windows; do but prove the wombs,
That bred them, graves: when they were born, they died,
    That had no muse to make their fame abide.
How many equal with the Argive Queen,
    Have beauty known, yet none so famous seen?   50
Achilles was not first, that valiant was,
    Or, in an army's head, that, lock'd in brass,
Gave killing strokes. There were brave men, before
    Ajax, or Idomen, or all the store,
That Homer brought to Troy; yet none so live:
    Because they lack'd the sacred pen, could give
Life unto'em. Who heav'd Hercules
    Unto the stars? Or the Tyndarides?
Who placed Jason's Argo in the sky?
    Or set bright Ariadne's crown so high?   60
Who made a lamp of Berenice's hair?
    Or lifted Cassiopea in her chair?
But only poets, rapt with rage divine?
    And such, or my hopes fail, shall make you shine.
You, and that other star, that purest light,
    Of all Lucina's train; Lucy the bright.
Than which, a nobler heaven itself knows not.
    Who, though she have a better verser got,
(Or poet, in the court account) than I,
    And, who doth me (though I not him) envy,   70
Yet, for the timely favours she hath done,
    To my less sanguine muse, wherein she hath won
My grateful soul, the subject of her powers,
    I have already us'd some happy hours,
To her remembrance; which when time shall bring
    To curious light, to notes, I then shall sing,
Will prove old Orpheus' act no tale to be:
    For I shall move stocks, stones, no less than he.

Then all, that have but done my muse least grace,
    Shall thronging come, and boast the happy place   80
They hold in my strange poems, which, as yet,
    Had not their form touch'd by an English wit.
There like a rich, and golden pyramid,
    Borne up by statues, shall I rear your head,
Above your under-carved ornaments,
    And show, how, to the life, my soul presents
Your form impress'd there: not with tickling rhymes,
    Or commonplaces, filch'd, that take these times,
But high, and noble matter, such as flies
    From brains entranc'd, and fill'd with ecstasies;   90
Moods, which the god-like Sidney oft did prove,
    And your brave friend, and mine so well did love.
Who wheresoe'er he be — (on what dear coast,
    Now thinking on you, though to England lost,
For that firm grace he holds in your regard,
    I, that am grateful for him, have prepar'd
This hasty sacrifice, wherein I rear
    A vow as new, and ominous as the year,
Before his swift and circl'd race be run,
    My best of wishes, may you bear a son.)   100

XIII   *Epistle to Katherine, Lady Aubigny*

'Tis grown almost a danger to speak true
    Of any good mind, now: there are so few.
The bad, by number, are so fortified,
    As what they've lost t'expect, they dare deride.
So both the prais'd, and praisers suffer: yet,
    For others' ill, ought none their good forget.
I, therefore, who profess myself in love
    With every virtue, wheresoe'er it move,
And howsoever; as I am at feud
    With sin and vice, though with a throne endu'd;   10

And, in this name, am given out dangerous
    By arts, and practice of the vicious,
Such as suspect themselves, and think it fit
    For their own cap'tal crimes, t'indict my wit;
I, that have suffer'd this; and, though forsook
    Of Fortune, have not alter'd yet my look,
Or so myself abandon'd, as because
    Men are not just, or keep no holy laws
Of nature, and society, I should faint;
    Or fear to draw true lines, 'cause others paint: 20
I, madam, am become your praiser. Where,
    If it may stand with your soft blush to hear,
Yourself but told unto yourself, and see
    In my character, what your features be,
You will not from the paper slightly pass:
    No lady, but, at some time, loves her glass.
And this shall be no false one, but as much
    Remov'd, as you from need to have it such.
Look then, and see yourself. I will not say
    Your beauty; for you see that every day: 30
And so do many more. All which can call
    It perfect, proper, pure, and natural,
Not taken up o'the doctors, but as well
    As I, can say, and see it doth excel.
That asks but to be censur'd by the eyes:
    And, in those outward forms, all fools are wise.
Nor that your beauty wanted not a dower,
    Do I reflect. Some alderman has power,
Or coz'ning farmer of the customs so,
    T'advance his doubtful issue, and o'er-flow   40
A prince's fortune: these are gifts of chance,
    And raise not virtue; they may vice enhance.
My mirror is more subtle, clear, refin'd,
    And takes, and gives the beauties of the mind.
Though it reject not those of Fortune: such
    As blood, and match. Wherein, how more than much

111

Are you engaged to your happy fate,
  For such a lot! That's mix'd you with a state
Of so great title, birth, but virtue most,
  Without which, all the rest were sounds, or lost.   50
'Tis only that can time, and chance defeat:
  For he, that once is good, is ever great.
Wherewith, then, madam, can you better pay
  This blessing of the stars, than by that way
Of virtue, which you tread? What if alone?
  Without companions? 'Tis safe to have none.
In single paths, dangers with ease are watch'd:
  Contagion in the press is soonest catch'd.
This makes, that wisely you decline your life,
  Far from the maze of custom, error, strife,   60
And keep an even, and unalter'd gait;
  Not looking by, or back (like those, that wait
Times, and occasions, to start forth, and seem)
  Which though the turning world may dis-esteem,
Because that studies spectacles, and shows,
  And after varied, as fresh objects goes,
Giddy with change, and therefore cannot see
  Right, the right way: yet must your comfort be
Your conscience, and not wonder, if none asks
  For truth's complexion, where they all wear masks.   70
Let who will follow fashions, and attires,
  Maintain their liegers forth, for foreign wires,
Melt down their husbands' land, to pour away
  On the close groom, and page, on New Year's Day,
And almost, all days after, while they live;
  (They find it both so witty, and safe to give.)
Let 'em on powders, oils, and paintings, spend,
  Till that no usurer, nor his bawds dare lend
Them, or their officers: and no man know,
  Whether it be a face they wear, or no.   80
Let 'em waste body, and state; and after all,
  When their own parasites laugh at their fall,

112

May they have nothing left, whereof they can
   Boast, but how oft they have gone wrong to man:
And call it their brave sin. For such there be
   That do sin only for the infamy:
And never think, how vice doth every hour,
   Eat on her clients, and someone devour.
You, madam, young have learn'd to shun these shelves,
   Whereon the most of mankind wrack themselves,   90
And, keeping a just course, have early put
   Into your harbour, and all passage shut
'Gainst storms, or pirates, that might charge your peace;
   For which you worthy are the glad increase
Of your blest womb, made fruitful from above,
   To pay your lord the pledges of chaste love:
And raise a noble stem, to give the fame,
   To Clifton's blood, that is deni'd their name.
Grow, grow, fair tree, and as thy branches shoot,
   Hear, what the muses sing about thy root,   100
By me, their priest (if they can aught divine)
   Before the moons have fill'd their triple trine,
To crown the burthen which you go withall,
   It shall a ripe and timely issue fall,
T'expect the honours of great Aubigny:
   And greater rites, yet writ in mystery,
But which the Fates forbid me to reveal.
   Only, thus much, out of a ravish'd zeal,
Unto your name, and goodness of your life,
   They speak; since you are truly that rare wife,   110
Other great wives may blush at: when they see
   What your tri'd manners are, what theirs should be.
How you love one, and him you should; how still
   You are depending on his word, and will;
Not fashion'd for the court, or strangers' eyes;
   But to please him, who is the dearer prize
Unto himself, by being so dear to you.
   This makes, that your affections still be new,

And that your souls conspire, as they were gone
   Into each other, and had now made one.   120
Live that one, still; and as long years do pass,
   Madam, be bold to use this truest glass:
Wherein, your form, you still the same shall find!
   Because nor it can change, nor such a mind.

XIV   *Ode to Sir William Sidney, on his Birthday*

   Now that the hearth is crown'd with smiling fire,
      And some do drink, and some do dance.
          Some ring,
          Some sing,
      And all do strive t'advance
   The gladness higher:
      Wherefore should I
      Stand silent by,
        Who not the least,
         Both love the cause, and authors of the feast?   10
   Give me my cup, but from the Thespian well,
      That I may tell to Sidney, what
          This day
          Doth say,
      And he may think on that
   Which I do tell:
      When all the noise
      Of these forc'd joys,
        Are fled and gone,
         And he, with his best genius left alone.   20
   This day says, then, the number of glad years
      Are justly summ'd, that makes you man;
          Your vow
          Must now
      Strive all right ways it can,
   T'out-strip your peers:

Since he doth lack
    Of going back
        Little, whose will
            Doth urge him to run wrong, or to stand still.   30
Nor can a little of the common store,
    Of nobles' virtue, show in you;
                Your blood
                So good
    And great, must seek for new,
And study more:
        Not weary, rest
        On what's deceas'd.
            For they, that swell
                With dust of ancestors, in graves but dwell.   40
'Twill be exacted of your name, whose son,
    Whose nephews, whose grand-child you are;
                And man
                Will, then,
    Say you have follow'd far,
When well begun:
        Which must be now,
        They teach you, how.
            And he that stays
                To live until tomorrow hath lost two days.   50
So may you live in honour, as in name,
    If with this truth you be inspir'd,
                So may
                This day
    Be more, and long desir'd:
And with the flame
        Of love be bright,
        As with the light
            Of bonfires. Then
                The birthday shines, when logs not burn, but
                                                men.   60

115

Good, and great God, can I not think of thee,
　　But it must, straight, my melancholy be?
Is it interpreted in me disease,
　　That, laden with my sins, I seek for ease?
O, be thou witness, that the reins dost know,
　　And hearts of all, if I be sad for show,
And judge me after: if I dare pretend
　　To aught but grace, or aim at other end.
As thou art all, so be thou all to me,
　　First, midst, and last, converted one, and three;　　10
My faith, my hope, my love: and in this state,
　　My judge, my witness, and my advocate.
Where have I been this while exil'd from thee?
　　And whither rapt, now thou but stoop'st to me?
Dwell, dwell here still: O, being everywhere,
　　How can I doubt to find thee ever, here?
I know my state, both full of shame, and scorn,
　　Conceiv'd in sin, and unto labour born,
Standing with fear, and must with horror fall,
　　And destin'd unto judgment, after all.　　20
I feel my griefs too, and there scarce is ground,
　　Upon my flesh t'inflict another wound.
Yet dare I not complain, or wish for death
　　With holy Paul, lest it be thought the breath
Of discontent; or that these prayers be
　　For weariness of life, not love of thee.

Notes

III   9 *termers*   visitors to London during Inns of Court terms;
       12 *Bucklersbury*   to wrap up groceries
V   title *Union* of Scotland and England under James VI and I
VII   3 *hothouse*   bath-house
XII   1 *squires*   pandars; 11 *ordinaries*   taverns; 21 *cockatrice*
       whore; 24 *pocky*   with venereal disease
XIII   2 *Aesculape*   god of medicine
XIV   title   See Introduction
XVII   6 *tree*   the laurel, into which Daphne was transformed
       to escape the lustful Apollo
XVIII   title *Mere*   wholly
XIX   1 *Cod*   perfume-bag
XXI   6 *bastinado*   beating with a stick
XXIII   1 *Phoebus*   Apollo, god of poetry
XXV   4 *Ganymede*   homosexual partner; 4 *cucqueen*   female
       cuckold
XXVIII   1 *Surly*   proud, arrogant; 4 *with...nose*   sneeringly;
       7 *tympanies*   tumours
XXIX   3 *device*   picture with motto
XXXII   .3 *Belgia*   the Benelux region, religiously divided; 10
       serenes   cool evening dampness
XXXVII   1 *Chev'ril*   pliable leather
XLI   1 *Gypsy*   deceitful woman
XLIV   1 *Chuff*   churl
XLV   title   See Introduction
XLVI   3 *band*   bond
L   2 *clysters*   pipes
LI   6 *gratulate*   celebrate
LIII   2 *pill'd*   compiled; 9 *motley*   jester's costume
LIV   title   See XXXVII and note; 2 *Star Chamber*:   preroga-
       tive law-court
LV   title   See Introduction

117

LVI 3 *brocage* cast-offs

LVIII 6 *points* punctuation/meaning

LIX title See Introduction re LIX-LXV

LXVI 12 *Broeck, Ruhr* 'The castle and river near where he was taken' (Jonson's own note)

LXIX title Obstinate Ball

LXXIII 5 *In primis* in the first place; 9 *Babylonian* confused; 13 *partie-per-pale* divided by a perpendicular stripe (heraldic); 15 *imprese* emblem; 20 *vein* style/vanity

LXXIV 9 *virgin* Astraea, goddess of justice

LXXV 3 *Paul's* St Paul's Cathedral

LXXVI 9 *facile* affable; 15 *rock* distaff (the line refers to the emblems of the Fates)

LXXVIII 1 *stall* theatre

LXXIX 2 *father* Sir Philip Sidney; 6 *issue* *The Arcadia*

LXXX 1 *ports* gates; 2 *meeds* deserts

LXXXI 4 *wealthy* trustworthy

LXXXII 2 *cast* dismissed

LXXXVII 1 *punk* whore

LXXXVIII 10 *disease* syphilis; 15 *motion* mechanical dummy; 16 *Paul's* St Paul's Cathedral, a place of fashionable resort

XCI 9 *prosecute* follow

XCII chapmen traders; 16 *gazetti, Gallo-Belgicus* news sheets; 19 *Star Chamber* prerogative law-court; 21 *mart* market; 23, 24 *Rimee, Bill* booksellers; 25 *Porta* Giovanni Baptista Porta, author of a book on cryptography; 30 *States* the Netherlands; 35 *Brethren* puritans

XCV 2 *doctrine* metempsychosis or transmigration of souls; 9 *proper* personal gift; 28 *apt* make fitting

XCVI 8 *better stone* white or fortunate stone, mark of approval; 10 *puisnees* juniors

XCVII title probably, like CXV and CXXIX, an attack on Inigo Jones; see Introduction; 1 *motion* puppet-show; *fading* Irish dance; 10 *bawdy stock* brothels; 14 *neadd* pp of need?

CI 8 *cates* food; 9 *rectify* remove impurities from; 13 *coney* rabbit; 30 *Mermaid* famous tavern; 36 *Pooly, Parrot* spies?

CII   12 *discerns*   distinguishes

CIII   2 *twilight*   early light; 7 *imprese*   emblem

CV   11 *Idalian Queen*   Venus; 15 *stile*   writing implement, symbol of Pallas/Minerva's wisdom; 20 *age before*   Golden Age

CVII   21, 22 *Villeroys, Silleries, Janins*   French statesmen; 25-26 *Hanou...Boutersheim*   mixture of real names and insulting coinages

CX   2 *west parts*   Gaul and Britain; 6 *stile*   writing implement; 14 *parts*   factions

CXI   9 *grutch*   grudge; 11 *deprave*   disfigure

CXII   4 *rank setting*   excessive betting; 22 *make thee prime*   give you a winning hand at cards

CXV   title   See note to XCVII; 26 *dore*   trick/disguise; 27 *Iniquity*   Vice in old miracle plays (punning on Inigo); 31 *engineer*   maker

CXIX   4 *prease*   press/crowd

CXX   title, *S.P.*   Salomon Pavy, child actor; 15 *Parcae*   Fates

CXXV   1 *first times*   Golden Age

CXXVI   8 *Daphne*   See note to XVII, line 6

CXXIX   title   See note to XCVII; 12 *babion*   baboon; *brave* ruffian; 16 *Cokely, Pod*   jesters/fools

CXXX   title *Ferrabosco*   lutenist and composer; 12 *spheres* cosmic spheres

CXXXII   6 *confer*   compare

CXXXIII   3 *Latin muse*   Virgil; 4 *knight*   Aeneas; 7-8 *Styx, Acheron, Cocytus, Phlegeton*   rivers in Hades; 8 *one*   River Fleet; 20 *adventer*   adventure; 28 *three for one*   dividends on profits; 30 *shoon*   shoes; 34 *embassage*   commission; 36 *dance...Norwich*   Will Kemp, famous comedian; 48 *Sybil, golden bough*   references to Aeneas's descent to Hades in *Aeneid* VI; 50 *Alcides*   Hercules; 62 *Ycleped* archaism for 'called'; 75 *sink*   sewer; 80, 81, 83 *Chimera, Briareus, Hydra*   famous monsters; 84 *trull*   Scylla; 85 *lighter*   barge; 89 *'How...place'*   What is the place called? 95 *ab excelsis*   from on high; 96 *Paracelsus*   famous alchemist; 102 *cataplasms* plasters; 115 *sough* sigh; *lurden* useless weight; 118 *Kate Arden* famous whore; 120 *foist* barge/foul smell (pun); 133 *nare* nostril; 155 *Tiberts* cats; 166 *peason* peas; 167 *meat* food; 177 *three...heads* Radamanthus, Aeacus, Minos (an inn-sign?); 180 *Madam Caesar* brothel-keeper; 190 *purblind fletcher* completely blind arrow-maker; 196 *him...A-JAX* Sir John Harington, author of a witty treatise on the water-closet (= jakes; hence A-JAX)

THE FOREST

II title home of the Sidney family; 2 *touch* black marble; 14 *birth* Sir Philip Sidney; 23 *kine* cattle; 25 *conies* rabbits; 36 *Officiously* dutifully; 48 *clown* peasant; 50 *suit* request to make; 73 *livery* provision; 77 *prince* Henry, Prince of Wales; 79 *Penates* household gods; 91 *lord* Robert Sidney, Viscount Lisle, later Earl of Leicester
III 44 *mast* acorn-eating; 47 *Sylvan* woodland deity; 48 *Comus* god of revelry; 50 *reign* the Age of Gold; 61 *leese* lose
IV 24 *gyves* chains; 36 *gins* traps; 56 *grutch* complain
V title See Introduction
VI 22 *pin'd* pained
VIII 3 *enow* enough; 10 *Spittles* leper-hospitals; *pest-house* plague hospital; 31 *emp'rics* quacks; 33 *Talc* cosmetics; 38 *stew* brothel; 39 *entail* bequeath
X 7 *cart* chariot; 10 *lord* Bacchus; 14 *smith* Hephaestus/Vulcan; 17 *trine* the Graces; 19 *son* Cupid; 24 *riffle* raffle; *Petasus* his characteristic broad-rimmed hat; 25 *ladies* the muses; 28 *commission* command; 30 *epode* lyric metre, alternating long and short lines
XI 9 *ports* gates; 69 *luxury* lust; 73 *sparrows* emblems of sensuality; 74 *turtles* turtle-doves, emblems of chastity; 115 *object* present
XII 22 *guilt* gilt (pun); 24 *Astraea* goddess of justice; 29

quarter-face turning away in aversion; 31 *father* Sir Philip Sidney; 43 *glorious* boastful; 44 *touch* black marble; 49 *Queen* Helen of Troy; 58 *Tyndarides* Castor and Pollux; 66 *Lucina* Queen Elizabeth; *Lucy* the Countess of Bedford; 68 *verser* possibly Michael Drayton; 90 *ecstasies* rapturous thoughts; 92 *friend* the Earl of Rutland (see Note on the Text); 98 *ominous* omen-bearing

XIII 25 *slightly* slightingly; 33 *taken up* bought from; 39 *coz'ning...customs* cheating tax-collectors; 72 *Maintain... wires* keep agents abroad to supply the newest fashions; 102 *triple trine* nine months

XIV 11 *Thespian well* from the muses; 42 *nephew* Sir Philip Sidney; *grand-child* Sir Henry Sidney

XV 5 *reins* seats of passion; 24 *Paul* Romans 7:24